THE DEVELOPMENT
OF
THE UNITED STATES

FROM COLONIES TO A WORLD POWER

By

MAX FARRAND

Professor of History in Yale University

BOSTON AND NEW YORK
HOUGHTON MIFFLIN COMPANY
The Riverside Press Cambridge

Published October 1918

TWELFTH IMPRESSION, FEBRUARY, 1925

The Riverside Press
CAMBRIDGE · MASSACHUSETTS
PRINTED IN THE U.S.A.

TO
THE ALLIES
In the Hope of a Better
Understanding

PREFACE

FOR over thirty years a new spirit has been gradually making its way into the study and interpretation of American history and taking other than political and military events into consideration. After the appearance of Bryce's *American Commonwealth* (1888), when instituting a comparison of this work with de Tocqueville's, Émile Boutmy wrote: "En un mot les États-Unis sont avant tout une société économique; ils ne sont qu'à titre secondaire une société historique et politique." McMaster's *History of the People of the United States* (1883) and Roosevelt's *Winning of the West* (1889) were indicative of the new history, while the greatest influence upon recent study has been exerted by Professor Frederick J. Turner through his classes and in his writings. Of the latter none has been more important than "The Influence of the Frontier in American History," which appeared in the *Annual Report* of the American Historical Association for 1893.

When the traditional, or conventional, point of view is once departed from, the most conspicuous, as well as the most significant, feature of American history becomes the expansion of a few thousand colonists, scattered along the Atlantic coast in the early seventeenth century, into a population of over one hundred millions, occupying the whole central portion of the North American continent and holding many outlying possessions. These people have developed distinctive traits and institutions that have become known as American, and if they do not constitute a nation they are at least citizens of a single great federal state, the United States of America. The original colonists were the subjects of European monarchs, and they have been joined by millions of people of all races and nationalities, mainly from monarchical states, yet they established and have maintained not the purest but the greatest democracy the world has known. From humble beginnings they have risen to a commanding position in the realm of industry and finance, and they have become one of the leading powers of the world.

The new history attempts to explain these things, and to that end many studies have been made and a large number of monographs produced, which are known to the special student but not to the general public. A new interpretation of American history has arisen which, at least to the prejudiced eyes of the present generation, offers a better understanding of the development of the United States, and should be of especial value to those whose interest in American history has been recently stimulated. In the hope of rendering a service to them this little book has been written. No one appreciates better than the author the difficulty of trying to compress the history of the United States into a small compass, but the appeal was too strong to be resisted, and he only hopes that his sins of omission are greater than those of commission. He has tried to state things truly, but even if he had succeeded he realizes that it would only be a part of the truth, for after all this is not intended to be comprehensive, it is only a sketch or rather an attempt to point out some of the things which help to explain how Americans have come to be what they are to-day.

As is the case with every historical study, and peculiarly so with one of this sort, the personal element of selection and emphasis has been the controlling factor. The work is in a sense a compilation, for the author has drawn freely upon books and men for his ideas and for the expression of them, and even the bibliography is a personal one, chosen largely from the books in his own library. He has tried to acknowledge the source of each extract, and wherever possible it has been done, but in default of that he would express here his gratitude to all from whom he has received assistance. He recognizes a peculiar obligation to Professor Turner, who, by his writings and even more by the generous sharing of his studies, brought the author to a realizing sense of the significance of the new point of view and has since assisted him in many ways. He is also under special obligations to President Arthur T. Hadley of Yale and to his former colleague the late Professor Guy S. Callender for stimulating suggestions obtained in friendly intercourse as well as from their books. He is grateful to his colleagues in American history Professor Charles M. Andrews and Professor Allen Johnson, who have both aided and encouraged him. The former rendered a special service which is recognized, though inadequately, in the bibliographical note at the end of Chapter I, and the latter read the manuscript of the first ten chapters and made helpful criticisms. Finally his thanks are due to his secretary, Miss Helen E. Williams, for her patient and untiring assistance.

M. F.

August 27, 1918.

CONTENTS

THE DEVELOPMENT OF THE UNITED STATES

FROM COLONIES TO A WORLD POWER

CHAPTER I

COLONIZATION

BECAUSE it was regarded as the beginning of all things every rightly constructed history of the United States used to commence with the discovery of the New World by Columbus in 1492. Recent writers, however, without meaning to detract from the glory or the achievements of the Great Admiral, hasten to point out that America would have been discovered if Columbus had never sailed. They cite as proof of this Cabral's voyage to India in 1500 when, in sailing for the Cape of Good Hope, that mariner was blown not so very far out of his course and touched the coast of Brazil. Some also refer to the tradition current among the descendants of old settlers in Newfoundland to-day, that when John Cabot sailed from England in 1497 he "discovered" only lands of which he had previously learned from Jersey fishermen. It is the incidental character of the discovery that is emphasized so cleverly in the assertion "that America was never sought, but stumbled on; that when found it was not wanted; that much of its exploration was due to a persistent effort to find a way around it."

Spanish occupation following the voyage of Columbus did not amount to much for nearly thirty years, when the unexpected discovery of stores of gold in Mexico, and afterwards in Peru, led to extensive and permanent colonization in the south. Such easily acquired riches influenced other countries and undoubtedly stimulated them to share in taking possession of the New World, but colonization would, nevertheless, have come about in other ways. Whether or not Cabot was preceded by Jersey fishermen, he was promptly followed by them and by Portuguese and French as well, so it could be said that as early as 1500 St. John's harbor in Newfoundland was well known to European fishermen.

Among the more romantic and spectacular happenings of the sixteenth century, the humble industry of fishing has been too little regarded, but it was of enough importance then to have special measures taken to encourage it. Protestant England, for example, found it desirable to reëstablish Catholic fast days with their abstinence from meat, and to that end issued a whole series of ordinances and proclamations. That there should be no misunder-

2

standing, the very first of these, an ordinance of Edward VI in 1548, averred, "that one daye or one kynde of Meate of it selfe is not more holie more pure or more cleane then an other"; but "that due and godlye astynence ys a meane to vertue and to subdue mens Bodies to their Soule and Spirite, and consideringe also spe-ciallye that Fysshers and men usinge the trade of lyvinge by fysshinge in the Sea, may thereby the rather be sett on worke," abstinence from meat in Lent and on other specified days was duly ordered, and heavy penalties imposed for disregard of the injunction. Apparently this proved to be worth while, as the number of these days was gradually extended, and a cen-tury later, it is said, over one hundred and forty days of each year were set aside on which the eating of flesh was forbidden. *

In the great development of the industry which followed these and other efforts the New-foundland fisheries played an important part, and they were gradually leading to a more per-manent occupation. Stations were established; the adjoining coasts were explored; and trading with the natives was becoming an organized business. The landing of the Pilgrim Fathers at Plymouth in 1620 is regarded as a great his-toric event, but some years earlier English fishermen and traders had appeared on the coast of Maine; it seems to be certain that fur-traders had agents who were living in the country all the year around; and so colonization in the north by both English and French inevitably would have resulted.

Colony planting
All of this means that forces were at work which probably would have produced somewhat the same results independently of individuals or particular incidents. But history is concerned with what actually happened, and the first permanent English settlement was made in Virginia in 1607. It was the work of a chartered trading company, and with all due allowance for other influences, it is safe to say that the primary interest of Englishmen, as well as of Europeans, in the planting of colonies was a commercial interest. In an age of expanding commerce and of international rivalry for control of the wonderful opportunities that were opening, this was as natural as it was inevitable, for there was a growing appreciation of the importance of these colonial enterprises in the extension of dominions. Other motives came into play, such as patriotism and religion, for the rendering of a service to his country or to his church, while he was advancing his own fortunes, appealed to the man of that time as it does at the present. But the main purpose underlying this colonial development was commercial.

4

Spain and Portugal had tried monopolies of government-controlled commerce; but among the rising commercial powers chartered joint-stock companies were favored for distant trading. England, Holland, France, Denmark, and Sweden established many such. Whether they are to be regarded as commercial companies or as colonizing companies depends upon the emphasis which is laid upon the one or the other phase of their activities. Under the auspices of these organizations and within a comparatively few years after Virginia, further English settlements were made in Bermuda, Massachusetts, Connecticut, and Rhode Island. At the same time the French had established themselves on the St. Lawrence and in the West Indies, the Dutch on the Hudson, the Swedes on the Delaware, and the Danes on the island of St. Thomas.

Another method that appealed especially to the British was colonization by proprietors, in which individuals or small boards took the place of the larger organizations. It was tried while the chartered commercial companies were still being formed and, seeming to offer an easier establishment and less trouble, it afterward practically superseded colonization by companies. In this manner came about the proprieties of Barbadoes and Maryland. When the Dutch colony of New Netherland was

5

seized by the English in 1664, it was turned over, with some adjoining territory, to the Duke of York as a propriety. The Duke immediately gave part of it, the Jerseys, to Sir George Carteret and Sir John Berkeley. Other colonies of this same type were the Carolinas, the Bahamas, and Pennsylvania.

Development The whole story of British colonial development is to be found in the adaptation of the colonists to their environment. The significant thing, and at the same time the most natural thing in the world, was that the colonists succeeded in ways not expected of them. Some colonial enterprises were started under delusions of easily acquired wealth, while all of the colonies were encouraged under hopes more or less false, and they succeeded only when the settlers, brought face to face with realities, adapted themselves to the conditions that were found.

The first necessity with which they were confronted was that of supporting life; the struggle for existence was not an easy one; it sometimes proved too much for them. The failures sink out of sight, and though the experience may have been useful and even necessary for those who survived, the record of success alone remains, or at any rate is of interest to the present. They lived — and ready sustenance was found for those who learned of the Indians to use the native grains and fruits in addition to the abundant fish and game.

Their next problem was to obtain some products that could be disposed of at a profit. By a process of natural selection the colonists found the things for which there was demand and they devoted themselves to the production of those without too great regard for British plans and prejudices. King James protested and the Government took measures against the growing of tobacco in Virginia. But when Captain John Smith, the picturesque adventurer and able leader who saved the colony from perishing in its early days, was questioned by a royal commission as to why Virginia did not grow wheat instead of tobacco, his simple reply was that a man's labor in tobacco cultivation was worth six times as much as it was in raising wheat. So the Southern Colonies devoted themselves primarily to the growing of tobacco, and later they added rice and indigo. The West India islands produced sugar, molasses, and rum, with a small amount of other commodities. In the North fishing had already proved itself to be a successful industry and source of profit, and to this was added lumbering and a varied agriculture. Of course, in all of the continental colonies furs were obtained in greater or less abundance.

In this way there came about a natural

grouping of the colonies according to their distinctive products: the bread colonies of New England, New York and Pennsylvania; the tobacco colonies of the South; the sugar colonies of the West Indies; and Africa should be added, whence came the negroes for the plantations. The elements were present for a flourishing commercial empire, and that is what developed. By the end of the seventeenth century British colonial establishments were over twenty in number, increasing to thirty in the following century, so that properly they should be regarded as parts of a great commercial empire stretching from Hudson Bay to the Caribbean, with outlying possessions in Asia and Africa.

The settlers The first essential in colony planting is to get settlers, and by their success in obtaining them the British proved their right to have and to hold a colonial empire. On the one hand were the colonies of which Virginia might be taken as the type, where for a long time they were willing to accept settlers "of any sort and on any terms," and where the need was so great, especially for labor, that compulsion was resorted to. On the other hand was New England, to which the migration was more largely voluntary, induced by political, religious, and social conditions in England. To all the colonies it was made easy for settlers to go, and many went on their own initiative with that irresistible impulse to seek a betterment of their fortunes or an improvement of their condition; in many cases, indeed, it meant to start life over again. For the average man no greater inducement could be offered than the opportunity to raise a crop or to obtain some products that could be exported and disposed of at a profit.

Another great incentive was religion; and in some of the colonies it was at times the greatest incentive of all. It was not the missionary zeal of the Spanish and French that drove them, but the opportunity to worship in one's own way that attracted men to the British colonies. This varied from the Puritans' establishment, of a state in which their own religion should be the one religion, to the asylums that were offered by Roger Williams in Rhode Island and William Penn in Pennsylvania, for the oppressed and religious discontented of all sects, of all creeds, and of every race.

Land Yet, after all, the greatest attraction was probably that of land. In a world whose political and social structure was based upon land-holding, and at a time when in older communities land was difficult, if not impossible, to obtain, it may readily be appreciated how dazzling the chance appeared

9

when a continent was to be given away. To the gentleman who wished to establish a landed estate, as well as to the common man whose desires were much more moderate, an unusual opportunity was offered. The Crown granted land lavishly to proprietors or to companies, and by them in turn it was freely granted to individuals.

In New England, with a few exceptions, the land was burdened with no feudal obligations. In the other colonies the declaration of fealty or the rendering of a nominal service was of little consequence in comparison with the required payment of a quit rent, no matter how small the amount might be. The objections to this form of tenure were so strenuous and the difficulty of collection proved so great that payment fell more and more into abeyance, and in some cases it was abandoned. The tendency was all in the direction of yielding more and more complete control to the holders and the ultimate result was the granting of land in full ownership. President Hadley, in his *Undercurrents in American Politics*, has pointed out that there is probably no greater or more significant difference between conditions in America and on the other side of the Atlantic than the acquisition of property, in which land is but a single item, in full ownership rather than under a feudal tenure.

The ease with which land could be obtained in America brought about a complication in colonial economy that materially affected the composition of the population, and the whole social structure as well. Men who could take up land for themselves and obtain all of the benefits of their own labor could not be expected or induced to work for others. Labor was a necessity; as it could not be secured voluntarily, it had to be obtained by compulsion. The form it happened to take was that of indentured service for a term of years. Large numbers of the immigrants could not pay their passage money, and such were then provided for if they would pledge their services for a number of years after arrival in the colonies. It was generally found that these indentured servants took up land and started out for themselves as soon as their term of service had expired. Accordingly there seemed to be only one way left to solve the labor problem, and that was by negro slavery. During the seventeenth century the number of slaves was relatively small, but with the failure of the white indentured servants and with the increasing demand for labor, negroes were brought in larger and larger numbers, until in the eighteenth century the importations were said to have reached to 10,000 and even to 20,000 a year.

Population
America became known as the land of opportunity and the population increased by leaps and bounds. Within the limits of the thirteen colonies, which later became the United States, in 1600 no settlers were to be found; at the end of twenty years there were 2500 and in twenty years more some 25,000; by 1700 the population was estimated at over 250,000; and before the middle of the eighteenth century the numbers ran up to over 1,000,000.

It was a heterogeneous mass that was thus assembled. Mingling with the English settlers from the start there had been some French, Germans, Swedes, Welsh, Scotch, Irish, and others, while the Dutch had formed a separate and not insignificant element by themselves. Then, toward the close of the seventeenth century, and in the eighteenth century, because of unsatisfactory conditions at home, Germans, Swiss, and Scotch-Irish poured into the colonies by tens, by hundreds, and by thousands. It was immigration on a scale proportionately greater even than the United States has seen in recent times. The Germans claim that by 1775 the people of their blood amounted to 225,000, or one tenth of the total population; and the Scotch-Irish claim 375,000, or about one sixth. Professor Edward Channing, in the second volume of his scholarly

History of the United States, has estimated that "About one third of the colonists in 1760 were born outside of America."

New England remained more largely peopled by English stock; the dominant planter class in the South was of similar origin, though negroes and white foreigners were there in great numbers; while the Middle Colonies contained the greatest admixture. Schoepf, a surgeon attached to some of the German mercenaries sent to America, could write from New York in 1780: —

A promiscuous crowd of almost all nations of Europe, of Jews and Negroes, of all creeds and sects, of people who have settled here for such diverse reasons, and often in order to escape legal penalties, here congregates and ingrafts upon the common country of their adoption the sentiments, manners, and habits of life which each individual has brought with him.

At about the same time Crèvecœur, in his delightful *Letters from an American Farmer*, being familiar with conditions in Pennsylvania and New York, answered his own question, "What is an American?", by saying: —

They are a mixture of English, Scotch, Irish, French, Dutch, Germans, and Swedes. From this promiscuous breed, that race now called Americans have arisen. . . . I could point out to you a family whose grandfather was an Englishman, whose wife was Dutch, whose son married a French woman, and whose present four sons have now four wives of different nations.

People who were going away from their own countries to settle in the New World, people who wished to leave home because they were unable to live under existing institutions, were usually allowed to do so without great difficulty. Reformers or even progressive members of a community may be estimable persons, but they are often unpleasant neighbors. The French Huguenots are rightly regarded as among the best elements of the population in the countries in which they settled; yet it was a relief to France at the time to have them go. The Scotch-Irish were competing dangerously with British industries, and advantage was taken of the difference in religious opinion to subject them, as Presbyterians, to the requirements of the Test Act which had been primarily intended for the subjection of Catholics. The Swiss Mennonites, because of their form of worship and their communistic tendencies, and also because of their refusal to bear arms, were considered a source of danger to both church and state. Governments could not sit idly by and allow these people, who were in general of an industrious class, to leave the country as freely as they chose. Laws were passed and proclamations were issued against emigration, but effective measures of enforcement were seldom taken. It is evident that underneath there was more or less of a feeling that after all it was "good riddance to bad rubbish."

The Americans were a nation of immigrants, a composite people, and the process of fusion was slow. While it was taking place thought and action were dominated by a relatively small upper class which was in general closely allied to the English by blood. This class fixed upon Americans the tradition of Anglo-Saxon origin which was probably not true for the majority of the people after the middle of the eighteenth century. Still the colonies were of English foundation; the English language was the dominant language; and the institutions were fundamentally British. This was well illustrated in the matter of government.

Government The New Englanders, in accordance with their training and traditions, but also in keeping with their environment, organized themselves into closely compact communities with a form of local life characteristic of the towns of Old England. While this implied a large amount of self-government, it did not mean popular control. For a time, in several of the colonies, the church and civil communities were practically identical and membership in the church was frequently required for the exercise of civil rights. This might be regarded as a restriction of political privileges, but it should rather be taken as an assurance of the equality of all men in the civil community just as they were equal before God in the church covenant. Yet theoretical considerations gave way before existing conditions; the aristocratic traditions of Old England were reproduced in America. Politically as well as socially the control of affairs remained largely in the hands of the upper class.

Local conditions in Virginia were responsible for the development in that colony of scattered private plantations with a small group of aristocratic owners in control of affairs, and a larger body of an inferior, and to a great extent dependent, class. It was, therefore, inevitable that the local government should take on a form of looser political organization than in New England. It accordingly followed the larger English divisions of hundreds and counties.

Other colonies showed variations and combinations of these types.

If the colonies are viewed in the light of their foundation as commercial enterprises, many things otherwise obscure seem relatively clear and simple. A joint-stock company would have a board of directors, the council, in London or wherever the company originated. The necessary authority in the colonies would naturally be exercised by a local or resident director, the governor, with an advisory board or committee, the council. As most of these enterprises did not prove to be successful business ventures, changes were made; and various experiments were tried in the effort to make them more profitable. For example, it was quickly appreciated that individual property-holding offered a great incentive to effort; accordingly mutual profit-sharing, which had been attempted in . the first colonies, was given up. The men upon the ground would know local conditions better; their experience would be helpful and their advice valuable; accordingly in Virginia each plantation or group of inhabitants was asked to send two delegates to an assembly — and representative government in America was begun. In Massachusetts advantage was taken of the fact that there was no stipulation in the charter that the meetings of the stockholders should be held in England. Accordingly, by taking the charter with them the settlers who were stockholders were able to hold meetings in the colony itself and so to obtain almost complete control of their own affairs.

The whole tendency was toward a greater and greater amount of self-government being allowed because it seemed to meet conditions better and because the colonies flourished under that arrangement. The colonies being of British foundation, the colonists being British subjects, and being granted all the rights and privileges of that status, it was natural that the institutions which developed should be essentially British. In practically every colony, therefore, the government developed on the British model. This consisted of a governor and council appointed by the Crown, as well as a whole set of officials holding their positions directly or indirectly by royal appointment, an assembly elected by the property-owners which had fairly extensive powers of legislation and taxation, and a series of judicial courts modeled on those of England.

Nor was this local self-government incompatible with the fact that before the end of the seventeenth century the Crown followed a fairly consistent policy of bringing all the colonies so far as possible under its own immediate control. The corporate colonies were continually giving trouble; the proprieties were only slightly better; simplicity and uniformity demanded royal administration. While it would be misleading to say that the Government never stopped until this purpose had been accomplished, it is true that with a few lapses the Government persisted in its purpose until out of some thirty establishments all but four eventually became royal or Crown colonies.

American Although colonial governments and institutions were essentially British, and though their development in the main followed on British lines, even governmental changes in England being reflected in America, yet in the adaptation to new conditions many and considerable modifications came about. Some of the most obvious as well as the most significant changes arose out of the mere growth of the colonies. A population that increased from 275,000 in 1700 to 1,200,000 in 1750 meant an expansion of settlement so rapid as to be phenomenal. While this was possible because of a liberal land policy, the expansion itself was partly responsible for that liberality. If the land were not freely given the impatient colonists seized it. James Logan, Penn's agent, complained in 1725 that there were "as many as one hundred thousand acres of land possessed by persons who resolutely set down and improve it without any right to it." [1]

A liberal land policy was a large factor in the establishment of property rights in America and this has been spoken of as one of the most significant features of American development; but there were social and political results from expansion that were of almost equal importance. Professor Frederick J. Turner, in his remarkable and telling articles on the West, beginning with *The Significance of the Frontier*

[1] With so great a demand for land there came an inevitable rise in land values and investment and speculation followed. In Philadelphia, in 1768, it was said that "every great fortune made here within these fifty years has been by land."

in American History, has pointed out that American expansion has been a process of colonization, and that the characteristic feature of American social development has resulted from starting life over again on the frontier. With the expansion of population and the development of new frontiers, came a constant recurrence of the process and a constant reorganization of social institutions. Being in operation from the earliest times this process slowly but surely was causing a divergence. The farther west the population went the farther removed were European influences, until out of the action and interaction of frontier and coast, out of the interplay of sections and of classes, there came something different, a development of life and institutions which has become known as *American.*

Where economic conditions were more nearly equal and where opportunities were open to all, social and political privileges could not be maintained on the same strict lines as in England. Many ambitious and discontented people in the settled portions of the colonies went of their own accord out to the undeveloped sections of the country and took up land. Other undesirable elements such as superfluous foreigners were pushed out to the frontier. Just as the American colonists in general were regarded by Englishmen and Europeans as of a somewhat inferior grade, so the frontiersmen were looked down upon by the coast settlers with something of indifference if not of contempt. The ruling classes in the colonies were running affairs in their own interests and without too great regard to the needs of others. They were fearful of the effect upon their hold of the social and political organization if this dissatisfied, rough, inferior element of the population should ever come into power. They accordingly took precautions to keep the reins of government in their own hands. The frontiersmen had many things to complain of, but their culminating grievance was that they did not have the share in the government to which they claimed their numbers entitled them, for then they would have been in a position to remedy the situation for themselves. Dissatisfaction existed everywhere, and just as soon as the discontented element was sufficiently strong to make trouble, trouble was bound to result. Continued friction, revolt, and even bloodshed forced concessions. Results were slow in coming, but ultimately the frontiersmen, the newcomers, the inferiors placed themselves on a footing of equality, at least so far as formal recognition was concerned, with the older, superior class.

Commerce and trade While England was yielding to her colonies a great deal of freedom in the matter of local government, she was passing many and minute regulations affecting the commerce and internal industrial development of those same colonies; and in this she was carrying out a fairly consistent policy and had done so from early times.

When the struggle with Spain in the sixteenth century, actuated by religious zeal as well as by lust for riches, was succeeded in the seventeenth century by a commercial rivalry with the Dutch, the control of the carrying trade became all-important. The famous series of Navigation Acts, beginning in 1651, unfolded a policy that was frankly intended to develop English shipping as the best support of the navy. Another closely related feature of the commercial policy developed in these and other acts was to promote in the colonies the production of naval stores for which England was dangerously dependent upon foreign countries with whom she might at any moment go to war. The colonies were also to provide raw materials which were not procurable at home, and they were to furnish a market for English manufactures, the exchange of commodities to be so regulated that the balance of trade would be in favor of the mother country.

In the maintenance of this commercial policy

it was inevitable that the Government should pass many laws, some of which were wise and some doubtless unwise, and many exceedingly irritating to the parties restrained by them. These annoying restrictions, however, were only parts or incidents in the organization of a great commercial empire. In this empire the interests of the mother country were paramount and those of the colonies subordinate, it is true; and where the two came into conflict the colonies must of course yield; but in general the interests of the two were not antagonistic, though at times they were divergent. England and her colonies were partners in a commercial organization. The prosperity of the one was dependent upon the prosperity of the other.

By their very location, with plenty of lumber and the finest of ship timbers, and under the stimulus which came from the fishing industry the New Englanders were foreordained to take up the building of ships. Not only did they build them for their own use; because of their cheapness and excellent qualities they were soon building them also for others. With sailors trained in the best of all schools, the fishing fleet, it was also foreordained that New Englanders should turn to carrying and trading. In all this development the requirement of the Navigation Acts that all ships must be English-owned and manned by English sailors was of great advantage, for the terms of the acts placed colonial and English shipping on the same footing.

The system of enumerated commodities by which specified articles could be shipped only to England worked something of a hardship, but compensation was made wherever possible. For example, in the case of tobacco, a better market could probably have been found on the Continent; but amends were made by granting a monopoly of the English markets. While some manufacturing was done for home use, it did not require legislation to restrain the colonists from this form of activity. In their stage of development they must of necessity rely very largely upon extractive industries. Such other commodities and manufactured articles as they could not or did not produce at home must be paid for out of the profits of the sales of their surplus products. In other words, the colonies were absolutely dependent upon outside markets.

The American continental colonies were carrying on their trade in a large measure for themselves. It was not a trade with the present methods of corporations, public carriers, and fixed routes. Its type was that of the individual merchant who carried his own goods, which would include cases where various people took shares in the venture and formed what might be called small joint-stock companies. There were some fairly well-established trade routes, as to England and to southern France and Spain, but the bulk of the trade, especially among the continental colonies themselves and between them and the West Indies, was carried on in a most irregular way. The colonies produced a great variety of commodities, and the methods of distribution were almost as varied as were the products. Professor Charles M. Andrews, in writing of the New England traders, each with a venture of only a few hundred pounds, going from colony to colony and to the West Indies, carrying every known commodity, well describes this as "a peddling and huckstering business."

The colonies found the markets which they required to a large extent in England and in Europe; in fact they traded all over the Atlantic and Mediterranean, and probably even on the Baltic coast. But the essential element in the prosperity of their trade was found in the West India islands. They could there dispose of lumber and foodstuffs to advantage; but it was of greater importance that a ready market was found for certain commodities which could not otherwise be sold. For example, the broken fish could not be offered in higher-class markets, but were in demand in the West Indies as food for the slaves. Part of this West India trade was thus equivalent to the profitable sale of by-products, and assisted the colonies materially in maintaining the balance of trade, which would otherwise have gone heavily against them.[1]

Early in the eighteenth century New England colonists found in the French West India islands molasses and other products so cheap and plentiful that it is said the planters were accustomed to throw much of them away. The trade which quickly sprang up worked to the detriment of the British islands, whose planters made complaint to Parliament. The sugar colonies, because of the greater profits from them, had always been favorites of the home Government, and the returned planters with their wealth exercised a peculiar social and political influence in England. Their appeal was accordingly listened to, and in 1733 the Molasses Act was passed which placed a pro-

[1] "The State of the Trade," as drawn up by the Boston merchants, recently printed by C. M. Andrews ("The Boston Merchants and the Non-Importation Movement," Colonial Society of Massachusetts, *Publications*, 1917, p. 167), shows this in most convincing fashion: ". . . about ⅔ of this Bank Fish turns out merchantable and is sent to Spain, Portugal, and Italy, the net proceeds of which with the freight is remitted to Great Britain; the other ⅓ being such as is over-salted, sunburnt, and broken, and thereby rendered unfit for any market in Europe is sent to the Islands in the West Indies, first to the English Islands, which cant consume more than ⅓, the remaining ⅔ is sent to the French foreign islands, in return for which we receive Molasses and a small proportion of ordinary sugars. This valuable branch of trade and nursery of seamen almost if not wholly depends on our trade to the foreign islands in the West Indies."

hibitive duty upon trade with the French islands.

In carrying on their diversified trade the colonists observed the regulations laid down by the mother country only so far as they were forced to. Exemptions from the requirements of the restrictive acts in the form of special licenses were oftentimes issued, and in many cases the laws were not rigidly enforced. So essential to the general prosperity of the empire was the prosperity of the New England trade, and so dependent was it in turn upon the trade with the French islands, that the Molasses Act was never strictly enforced.

There is no doubt that irregular trade or smuggling was carried on to a fairly large extent; even if it had not been tolerated by the British it would have been difficult to prevent on account of the great length of the colonial coast-line with its many bays and creeks which made careful patrol almost impossible. It has been said that the colonists smuggled whenever it was to their interest to do so; it is also said that the colonies flourished by reason of neglect. There may be an element of truth in these assertions, but the larger truth is that the colonies were flourishing with the rest of the British Empire, not in spite of the restrictive policy, but because they were a part of this great successful commercial organization. An important factor in colonial prosperity seems to have been that the lack of capital inevitable in an early stage of industrial development was to a large extent supplied by British credit. Many merchants in the colonies traded with the British merchants whose supply of capital enabled them to extend the necessary credit for the Americans to carry on their trade.

Rivalry with the French Expansion had brought the colonists into contact and into conflict with the Indians, which led to demands upon the home Government for more adequate provision for defense. Expansion also brought them into rivalry and into conflict with the French and led the colonists into taking a more and more important part in the plans of imperial expansion. When William III, immediately after his accession to the English throne in 1689, joined the Grand Alliance against Louis XIV, the American colonists took a minor part in what they called "King William's War." Again they shared in the War of the Spanish Succession, which they called "Queen Anne's War" (1701–1714), and in the War of the Austrian Succession (1740–1748), which they called "King George's War."

This was not merely a matter of duty on the

part of the colonists; self-interest required their participation. At first they were mostly concerned about the North Atlantic fisheries, and aggressive actions on their part were directed largely to the breaking of French and to the establishing of British control. The question continued to be a big factor in the years and in the wars that followed, but expansion brought the Americans and the British as well to a realization of the fact that there was a larger question involved, and that the rivalry between the French and British in America was actually a struggle for the possession of a continent. Military instinct, aided by the more or less accidental location of their first settlements upon the St. Lawrence, had shown the French the advantage of seizing the more important strategic points to control the interior of the continent, and had accordingly led them to establish a series of forts on the Mississippi, the Ohio, and the Great Lakes as well as on the St. Lawrence. On the other hand the British had characteristically encouraged settlement and as the middle of the eighteenth century was approaching they were organizing colonizing companies for the purpose of settling the Ohio Valley.

When the inevitable struggle in Europe was renewed in the Seven Years War (1756–1763), the fighting had already been going on in

America for over a year, growing out of the eagerness on the part of both contestants to seize the headwaters of the Ohio. The British continental colonies contained over a million souls, the French less than a hundred thousand. The outcome was a foregone conclusion; and as the war had begun, so before peace was reached in Europe the fighting had ended in America with the capture of Montreal by the British in 1760.

The changed character of the struggle in America, or at least the appreciation by the colonists of the importance of its issue to them, was shown by the fact that they no longer designated it as their sovereign's war, but as the "French and Indian War." Their self-interest was also shown by the fact that when their immediate aims seemed likely of achievement, when the headwaters of the Ohio were assured to their possession, and the fisheries were evidently to remain under their control, the colonists did not hesitate to engage in what should really have been regarded as treasonable trade with the enemy. They supplied the French with provisions which the British troops could have used, and they "cynically justified it on the ground that they were making money out of the enemy."

The result of the Seven Years War is a matter of world history. As it marked an epoch in British imperial development, it also marked an epoch in American history. The French lost practically all of their American colonies. Louisiana was given to Spain in compensation for Florida, which had been yielded to the British in exchange for Cuba. Canada and adjoining territories went to Great Britain, and only two little islands off the coast of Newfoundland were left to France for the use of her fishermen.

BIBLIOGRAPHY

Modern historical works generally contain bibliographical notes upon their respective subjects, but it is often desirable to use something more comprehensive. For this purpose, the most convenient is Channing, Hart and Turner, *Guide to the Study and Reading of American History* (1912). J. N. Larned, *Literature of American History* (1902) has the advantage of a critical comment upon each title noted. More recent publications can be followed in *Writings on American History* (published annually).

Among the students of American colonial history Professor Charles M. Andrews, of Yale University, seems to grasp with a constantly widening comprehension the whole colonial period of American history, in its external relations as well as in its internal development. His views have been only partially presented in printed works, among which might be noted as of general interest: *Colonial Self-Government* (1904); *The Colonial Period* (1912); an article on "Colonial Commerce" in the *American Historical Review* (1914–1915); *The Fathers of New England* (1919); and *Colonial Folkways* (1919). The author is greatly indebted to his colleague, having made free use of his ideas both published and unpublished, for Professor Andrews has been kind enough to discuss with the writer several of the points made in this and the following chapter, and to allow him to use the manuscript of a lecture delivered at the Lowell Institute, October, 1916, containing a brief summary of colonial history.

H. L. Osgood and G. L. Beer have placed all students under obligations to them by their works on the American Colonies, and the British Colonial System, but their writings would hardly be considered popular. Of the printed narrative ac-

31

counts probably the best is Edward Channing's in the first three volumes of his scholarly *History of the United States* (1905–1912). A short and readable narrative is C. L. Becker's *Beginnings of the American People* (1915). European conditions, the discoveries and explorations are well described in E. B. Cheyney, *European Background of American History* (1904), and E. G. Bourne, *Spain in America* (1904). Excellent detailed bibliographies are to be found in all of these works. Edward Eggleston, *Beginners of a Nation* (1896) and *Transit of Civilization from England to America* (1901) are interesting and illuminating.

There is no comprehensive work on the land system in the colonies. Upon the population, to be recommended are: A. B. Faust, *German Element in the United States* (2 vols., 1909); C. K. Bolton, *Scotch-Irish Pioneers* (1910); and H. J. Ford, *Scotch-Irish in America* (1915). C. M. Andrews, in *Colonial Folkways*, has some excellent sections developing the composite character of the American people. The author had a series of articles in the *New Republic* for December, 1916, making no pretense at scholarship, but drawing an interesting comparison with recent immigration to the United States.

In addition to his article on the frontier already referred to in the text, any study of colonial expansion must take into consideration F. J. Turner's "The Old West" (*Proceedings* of the Wisconsin Historical Society, 1908).

G. S. Callender, *Selections from the Economic History of the United States, 1765–1860* (1909), is not a book for the general reader, but it contains many extracts throwing light upon economic phases of American development and the short Introductions to the different chapters are brilliant interpretations that are full of suggestion. Recent publications of the Carnegie Institution, though not popular in character, are indispensable for their subjects: V. S. Clark, *History of Manufactures in the United States, 1607–1860* (1916); E. R. Johnson *et al.*, *History of Domestic and Foreign Commerce of the United States* (1915); and *History of Transportation in the United States before 1860*, edited by B. H. Meyer (1917).

The works of Francis Parkman (1865–1892), because they are both fascinating in interest and scholarly in character, still remain the standard history of the French in America and of the struggle between them and the English. The most recent accounts are William Bennett Munro, *Crusaders of New France* (1918), and George M. Wrong, *The Conquest of New France* (1918).

CHAPTER II

INDEPENDENCE

THE retention of Canada while returning the conquered West India islands to France, and the acceptance of Florida from Spain in return for Havana, indicated how important, in comparison with the West Indies, the continental colonies had grown in the estimation of the British. The immediate question was what was to be done with the newly acquired territories. It was answered by the Proclamation of 1763. This grouped the new territories into four provinces or governments, restricted, in all of the colonies, settlement to the east of the Alleghenies, and placed strict limitations upon those engaging in trade with the natives. Though tentative in character, the proclamation was intended to prevent friction with the Indians; it was intended for the conservation of the fur-trade; but it seems also to have been intended to keep the colonies within reach of imperial authority.

The new policy There seems to have been a growing realization on the part of the British as to the necessity of a better colonial organization and of a more effective administration. Events and experiences of the recent

33

war strengthened this into a conviction. The larger problem of imperial organization and control would probably have presented itself at about this time under any circumstances, but it was the acquisition of new territory which hastened the new policy. The very extent of the empire required a strengthening of the imperial bonds and a more adequate system of defense. It seemed only fair also that the financial burden thereof should be more equitably distributed.

The Proclamation of 1763 was not popular in the colonies, but it was acquiesced in as a temporary measure, which would be modified in the course of time to meet colonial needs. The other features of the new policy were more objectionable. In 1764 the Sugar Act was passed, which was ostensibly a modification of the Molasses Act of 1733, but revealed new purposes. It frankly stated that "it is just and necessary that a revenue be raised in America," although it smoothed over that declaration by adding that the revenue so raised should be used for the protection of the colonies themselves. In the earlier statute the duties were prohibitive and had been disregarded. In the new act lower duties were laid, but provision was made for their collection as well as for better enforcement of all the trade and navigation acts. Measures in this direction had been taken during the war to prevent trade with the enemy. But this was in times of peace, and pointed ominously toward a restriction of the freedom which the colonists were wont to enjoy. Accordingly they complained bitterly that the measure was unwise and unjust.

The revenue to be derived from the Sugar Act was relatively insignificant, and the next year, in spite of the protests and petitions of the colonists, a stamp tax was laid. The act required the affixing of stamps to all legal and commercial documents in the American colonies. The revenue therefrom, like that of 1764, was to be used in the protection of the colonies, and the proceeds of both together would meet only a part of the expense involved. This seems reasonable enough, but the train of events was started which ended almost inevitably in the revolt, and in the independence, of the continental colonies.

The quarrel With the large measure of self-government which the colonies had been allowed to develop, there had come frequent and unavoidable conflicts between the assemblies elected by the colonists and the administrative officers appointed by the Crown. In these contests the assemblies were gradually getting the better of it through 'ising the power of the purse, in good old English fashion, granting generously when concessions were made to them and thwarting other measures in which their "rights" had been disregarded. They were thus asserting and gradually establishing the principle of demand and supply. The levying of a tax as proposed in the Stamp Act was taking money directly from the colonists without giving them any voice or say in the matter. On the other hand the British insisted and believed that they were not interfering with the self-government of the colonies. Feeling that this legislation was for the benefit of the empire as a whole, Parliament naturally resented the blocking of large policies by what were regarded as petty or local, selfish interests.

Underneath all this was an important difference between American and British institutions. A candidate for election to the House of Commons might stand for any constituency and considered himself a representative of all the people. Owing to peculiar conditions in America a member of a legislative body was elected from the district in which he lived and represented primarily the interests of his own immediate section. Accordingly representation meant one thing in England, and quite another thing in America. Believing that they were legislating for the interests of the empire, Englishmen could not understand why the colonists had any ground for complaint, as they were no more unrepresented than were the majority of the people in England. The Americans could not see how they were represented at all.

A weakness in the colonial contention lay in the fact that the colonies by the very nature of their foundation and development had always been controlled by the acts of trade. One of the common incidents of those acts had been the laying of duties. To the principle of this the colonists had never objected. They were now bitterly opposed to the Stamp Act and there must be some justification for their opposition. This was not merely to furnish a plea; they had to justify their position to themselves. That justification was found in the assertion that while the British Government had the right to regulate matters of trade and commerce and might levy taxes for that purpose, which they called "external taxes," the government had no right to levy taxes for revenue, which were termed "internal taxes."

It is well recognized that constitutional arguments are always found in support of any opinion and especially to bolster up the opposition. That it is not unfair to regard the American reasoning in that light, is shown by simply quoting from James Madison, who later became the great authority on the Constitution of the United States. Shortly after the war was over he admitted: —

37

The line of distinction between the power of regulating trade and that of drawing revenue from it, which was once considered the barrier of our liberties, was found, on fair discussion, to be absolutely undefinable.

There is, therefore, ground for saying that taxation without representation was an excuse rather than the cause of the Revolution. The mere enforcement of the laws of trade, accompanied as it was with a few years of hard times, would probably have been sufficient to force the issue. If the colonists had reached a stage in their development where they seemed to require a greater freedom of trade than the British were willing to grant, they were justified in asserting their independence; but it will not do to inquire too closely into the reasons which they gave in the excitement of the struggle.

It must not be imagined that the colonists were in any sense hypocritical or insincere in the position which they had taken. They believed as firmly as could be believed that they were fighting the battle of English liberty, fighting for rights of Englishmen as old as Magna Carta. On the other hand Parliament was legally and constitutionally in the right. Whether Parliament acted in a wise or statesmanlike way is another matter. Tact rather than firmness was needed, and diplomacy rather

38

than obstinacy. Ignorance was a fault of both parties with, perhaps, the greater responsibility therefor resting upon the home Government. Like so many quarrels, this was one in which neither party understood the other's side of the question. So divergent were the points of view, that to try and reconcile them may have been hopeless, but it does seem that the American colonists, if they had been handled with tact, could have been led to meet their share of the expenses of government, although it might have been accomplished only at too great a sacrifice of imperial authority. It is an interesting speculation, however, that the United States of British America may not have been an impossibility.

It was a condition rather than any one cause that brought on the Revolution, and various forces were working to produce that condition. Considering how large a part religious freedom had had in American colonization, and how many of the colonists were dissenters, it may readily be appreciated how a movement for the establishment of an American episcopate would be regarded. This was the inauspicious moment that was chosen to agitate the subject anew and with unusual vigor. It was of course construed to be an effort on the part of the Crown not merely to control the religion of the people, but to control the clergymen, who were generally leaders in their communities and who had preached and spread ideals of liberty among their parishioners.

The personal element is always a difficult one to estimate, and yet such considerations have to be taken into account. All the conflicting passions that are aroused by hopes, ambitions, and interests; all the rivalries, jealousies, and suspicions — these are the forces which determine the attitude and the action of many men. A trivial illustration throws a flood of light upon this: When a sufficient number of years had elapsed to make such a confession possible, an American admitted that his grievance against England had been that he was "cut out with his sweetheart by a 'red coat gallant,' a marine officer with Lord Dunmore." Another, hearing this, said that a tax on tea was supposed to have caused the Revolution, but he had reason to believe that it was the Boston girls caring more for the British officers than they did for the Americans.

Declaration of Independence Other factors came into play, and opinions will necessarily differ as to the relative importance of each. It is merely a question of emphasis. Conditions being what they were, once started the five-act drama moved inexorably to its conclusion: Misunderstanding; Unwise Demands; Disobedience; Punishment; Rebellion.

Determined and united opposition brought about the repeal of the Stamp Act, but accompanied by a formal declaration of Parliament's right to tax, and when the raising of a colonial revenue was next attempted by the Townshend Acts in 1767, troops were unwisely sent over. Concerted action of the colonists again rendered the acts a failure, at least so far as revenue was concerned, and they were accordingly repealed; but there was a tax left upon tea and, as it was understood in the colonies to serve as an example, a boycott of that beverage became widespread and popular. Then, too, the presence of the troops in Boston led to constant bickering, until finally, in a brawl which developed into a riot, five citizens were killed, and Americans promptly magnified the incident into the "Boston massacre."

The colonists were now so excited that everything was misunderstood. In 1772 the East India Company, being in sore financial straits, took advantage of concessions by Parliament to offer bargain sales of tea in the colonies. The colonists took this as an effort to bribe them into paying a tax. In practically all the colonies the cargoes of tea were kept from sale, by force of public opinion if possible, by threats if necessary, and sometimes by violence. In Boston, where Governor Hutchinson had insisted upon having the tea landed, a mob of disguised men dumped the tea into the harbor. The fat was in the fire and the flames spread rapidly. Parliament could not overlook such flagrant disobedience and acts for the punishment of Boston were quickly adopted. The other colonies rallied to the support of Massachusetts; united action strengthened resistance; and the time for reconciliation had passed.

The Quebec Act, for the government and control of the recently acquired French provinces, happened to be passed at the same time that these extreme measures were taken for the punishment of Boston and Massachusetts in 1774. Harmless enough in itself, because of the company it was in every evil was ascribed to it. In accordance with treaty guarantees one of its provisions permitted the Roman Catholic inhabitants to worship after the forms they had been accustomed to. This was denounced as the beginning of an attempt to establish Popery and the dominion of the Roman Church over the colonies; in the clerical language of the time it was said that it "must have caused a Jubilee in Hell!" It is interesting to notice that one of Parliament's last attempts to compel submission was an act of 1775 cutting off the New England fisheries. Apparently it was felt to be as severe a punishment as could be inflicted.

When unity of action on the part of the

colonists became essential, accustomed as they were to representative self-government, and being adaptable by nature and by training, they readily found a way. They first established committees of correspondence for purposes of information and the interchange of ideas. Ultimately they came together in congresses of delegates from all the colonies. It was with apparent reluctance that they prepared to take the irrevocable step. But whatever may have been their misgivings, when the time was ripe the Continental Congress adopted the resolution "that these United Colonies are, and, of right, ought to be, Free and Independent States." This later was elaborated into the formal Declaration of Independence, and the Fourth of July became and has remained the great national holiday.

There seems to have been a dawning consciousness in the minds of some of the more thoughtful men in the colonies that it was impossible to deny the right of Parliament to legislate and even to tax as it might see fit. Accordingly, as in the Revolution of 1688, where justification was found in the assertion by the House of Commons, that James II had broken "the original contract between king and people," so Locke's theories were also resorted to by the colonies to justify the breach with the mother country. Relying on the same contract theory of the origin of government, it was asserted that after their arrival in this country, the colonists had, of their own accord, re-adopted the system of laws under which they had hitherto lived in the mother country, and that they were subjects of the British king because they had freely accepted him, and not because he was the chief magistrate of Great Britain.

Such was the fundamental principle underlying the Declaration of Independence as it was formulated by Thomas Jefferson. An instrument that was based upon such a patent misconception of historical facts must be regarded as somewhat in the nature of a declaration of principles by a political party. Yet because it was adapted to the necessities of an aroused and angry people, and because of the way in which it met the aspirations of the moment, it was a great document and a notable achievement. Nothing else could have served the purpose so well. Its practical charges appealed to the New Englanders; its theories appealed to the Virginia planters; and it obtained very general support.

The Revolution This does not mean that the Revolution was the work of a united people, nor that it represented a great popular uprising. It was inaugurated and carried through by a relatively small class.

Such a careful student as Dr. Samuel Eliot Morison recently estimated that out of a population of two and a half million, less than one third may have actively supported the American cause; over one half remained neutral; and at least 250,000 remained loyal to the British Crown.

In the absence of any general popular support, and with a government utterly incapable of compelling military service, it was necessary to rely upon volunteer soldiers and an inadequate local militia system. It was never possible, therefore, to keep a satisfactory army in the field. The Americans were fortunate in their commander-in-chief, George Washington. Better as a strategist than as a tactician, yet first-class as neither, he cannot be regarded as a great general. Hampered by the distrust and jealousy, as well as by the inability, of other officers, restricted by lack of soldiers, and weakened by the inefficient support from Congress, Washington's greatness as a leader shines all the more conspicuously.

Considering the weakness of the American forces it seems as though the rebellion should have been easily and quickly crushed. The failure to do so has been attributed to the half-hearted prosecution of the war by the British, to the mediocrity of their officers, to the use of mercenary troops, or to the inefficiency in supplying food, clothing, and ammunition. There may be something of truth in each of these criticisms, but the fact remains that considering the nature of the country and the means of transportation, it was difficult, if not impossible, "relentlessly to follow up the main body of the American army until it was captured or dispersed."

Even if the British had been successful in such an effort it is doubtful if the colonies could ever have been wholly subdued. Guerrilla warfare and irregular resistance might have been carried on almost indefinitely. On the whole the British were getting much the better of the struggle, and if, as was feared in America, the war had been brought to an end in 1780, by the intervention of European powers, a large part of the territory of the revolting colonies would have been in British hands. Apparently they were counting upon the colonists becoming tired of continuing the rebellion. But time was a factor working in favor of the Americans, rather than of the British.

It was under such conditions that the greatness of Washington as a leader was shown. In spite of discouragements and lack of support, with superhuman patience and an utter disregard of self-interest, he maintained the struggle, sometimes it appeared by the sheer strength of his will alone. By steadfastness of purpose, he rallied about him such elements as could be induced to follow him and kept up what frequently seemed to be a hopeless resistance. Whether or not he would have been finally successful in convincing the British that the fighting would be continued indefinitely, and that the subjection of the colonies could only be secured at too great a cost, is a matter of speculation only. The Americans won the Revolution with the support of the French. This support was not given with entirely altruistic motives. Many adventurous spirits and soldiers of fortune found the opportunity they were seeking in the American army. Benjamin Franklin's personality and picturesque appearance captured the Parisian imagination, and helped to render the American cause a popular one. The main purpose, however, of the French was to reëstablish France in the position of supremacy which she had held a generation before, and in this a weakening of the British Empire would be of advantage.

Secret and irregular assistance in money and supplies had been given from the start by both France and Spain, because of their antagonism to Great Britain, but such a situation could not continue indefinitely. When the Americans, partly through the mismanagement of a British plan of campaign and largely through the uprising of the frontiersmen in New York and Vermont, had succeeded in forcing the surrender of General Burgoyne and his army at Saratoga in 1777, the French came out openly on the side of the revolting colonies. The next year they entered into a formal alliance with the United States. The Spanish could not be persuaded to take the same stand. In 1779 they declared war against Great Britain, but without recognizing or joining the Americans.

The moral support of the French alliance was of great consequence, but the material assistance which they gave was of even more. As events turned out, the coöperation of the French might be regarded as the determining factor, because their fleet and troops made it possible to compel the surrender of Cornwallis at Yorktown in 1781. While a severe blow to the British, this was not disastrous from a military point of view. It was, however, decisive, because the British could not afford to carry on the war any longer. When the news reached England, on motion of General Conway the House of Commons resolved that it would "consider as enemies to his Majesty and this country all those . . . attempting the further prosecution of offensive war on the continent of North America, to the purpose of reducing the revolted colonies to obedience by force." Negotiations for peace were then seriously undertaken.

The settlement of the terms of peace was not a simple matter because there were so many interests involved. In so far as American affairs were concerned the greatest difficulty lay in Spain's designs on the western country. Having been given Louisiana by France in 1763, and having taken the Floridas in 1780, Spain wanted the region between the Alleghenies and the Mississippi River, so as to control the entire Mississippi Valley. France was under obligations to Spain for entering the war and, not having been able to obtain for her the promised Gibraltar, felt the necessity of supporting her other demands. Any French obligations to the United States were cancelled by the establishment of the latter's independence.

The American commissioners had been instructed to do nothing without the knowledge and approval of France. Fortunately for the United States they were broad-minded men, and when they perceived the drift of affairs, they disregarded instructions and came to terms directly with Great Britain. Difficulties over such questions as the payment of British creditors and the indemnification of Loyalists were as nothing in comparison with the previous obstacle of Spain's desires, and were ultimately adjusted. The main points in the treaty, which was finally ratified in 1783, were the recognition of the independence of the

United States and the establishment of her territorial limits from the Atlantic to the Mississippi and from Canada on the north to Florida on the south.

There is a very natural tendency on the part of Americans to glorify the Revolution, together with every one and every thing connected with it. The ultimate results are regarded as good because they have been so important in the later development of the United States. The Revolution undoubtedly stimulated the spread of democracy and helped greatly in separating church and state, and whether or not such things are inherently desirable is only an academic question, for they are established facts in American life. Yet such an attitude of mind overlooks the demoralizing effects of the Revolution. There was, of course, the usual profiteering, while speculation and extravagance, characteristic of war times, were probably enhanced by local conditions. In the complete demoralization of the country's finances there were enormous issues of paper money and a consequent depression of the currency. This bore heavily upon the more conservative propertied class, but offered an unusual chance for speculation. Fortunes were quickly made and almost as freely spent by people who were not accustomed to the use of money.

A more sinister aspect is found in the years and events preceding the establishment of independence. Owing to the difficulties in regard to taxation which led up to the Revolution, the Americans were developing an objection to any taxation at all, or at least to any which was seriously felt. In their efforts to prevent the enforcement of laws which they thought unconstitutional they used irregular and illegal methods, and even resorted to riots and other forms of violence. The unusual feature of it was that these things were justified by the leading citizens as being necessary and patriotic and therefore righteous. It was an unfortunate way for a people to begin their independent career.

BIBLIOGRAPHY

Almost enough has been written upon the American Revolution to form a library in itself. But on the whole nothing seems better than the summarized account in William E. H. Lecky's *England in the Eighteenth Century*, chap. XVII, published separately by D. Appleton & Co. (1910), as *The American Revolution*. The best recent account is in Channing's *History of the United States*, vol. III (1912). The most interesting narrative is that by Sir George Otto Trevelyan (*The American Revolution*, 4 vols., 1905–1913; concluded as *George The Third and Charles Fox*, 2 vols. 1912–1914).

In addition to the general titles mentioned in the bibliography of Chapter I should be noticed the readable narrative by Carl Becker, *The Eve of the Revolution* (1918). J. J. Jusserand has an interesting essay upon the French in the Revolution in his *Americans of Past and Present Days* (1916). Authoritative for its subject is C. W. Alvord, *The Mississippi Valley in British Politics, 1763–1774* (2 vols. 1917). Good but scarcely more than conventional accounts of both the causes leading up to the Revolution and the course of the fighting may be found in G. E. Howard's *Preliminaries of the Revolution* (1905); C. H. Van Tyne's *The American Revolution* (1905); and T. C. Smith's *Wars between England and America* (Home University Library, 1914).

If the author had been able to use it in the writing of this chapter, Arthur M. Schlesinger's scholarly study of *The Colonial Merchants and the Revolution* (1918) might have modified the expression of some of his ideas, though without materially changing his point of view.

CHAPTER III

THE UNITED STATES

LONG experience in managing their own affairs had grown into what might be called a habit of self-government, and the Americans reaped large benefits therefrom when the machinery of government was thrown out of gear by the Revolution. During the troubled years before the final breach, whenever the established order was interrupted, the colonists took things into their own hands. Usually an extra-legal body assumed control, and maintained not only the forms but the actual working of a government. The resolutions adopted and the actions taken by such bodies, although without the force of law, were generally recognized and obeyed by their constituents. Then, when independence was declared, each state formed a government of its own; not always immediately, where the old government answered the purpose, but in the course of three or four years. Certain phases of the evolution of the state governments are as interesting as they are important.

State constitutions
Practically all of the colonies had come into existence under formal charter grants. In some cases the charter had remained the ultimate authority

as to the rights and privileges which had been given. The colonists, therefore, had been accustomed to appeal to a definite and fixed instrument. Of equal and perhaps greater influence was the prevailing belief that government was founded by a compact; if the compact were written it ought to be so much the stronger. This theory of the origin of government was strengthened by the existence in the religious sphere of the church covenants. It was even changed into a conviction by the conditions in America; such compacts had actually been formed, as on board the Mayflower, and in the founding of Connecticut and New Haven. Accordingly, when the states came to set up their own establishments, in each case the government was carefully provided for in a written instrument, varying in length from one to twelve thousand words. Sometimes the constitution, as it was called, was framed and promulgated by the Revolutionary Congress of the state; sometimes by a body especially elected for that purpose. Only gradually did the idea evolve that these instruments should be submitted to the voters for approval.

This first series of written constitutions has always attracted a great deal of attention, but never more than when they were first adopted. It was an age when men were speculating upon political matters, and here was an experiment in self-government that might offer a solution of much-discussed problems. As soon as the last of the states had formed its government, in 1780, Congress printed a small edition of the constitutions, which was quickly reprinted and received wide circulation in Great Britain and on the Continent as well as in the United States.

But however interesting or valuable in political theory, these state constitutions were of more importance as practical working instruments of government, for they or their successors are in operation to-day in all the states of the Union, with, of course, the modifications that have been found necessary through the experience of nearly one hundred and fifty years. In that capacity the most significant thing is that so little difference can be found between the government under them and what it had been under the colonial charters. The constitutions did scarcely more than continue the forms, the offices, and the practices of the colonial régime, with a few changes in name rather than in substance. In fact, in the case of Connecticut and Rhode Island, the charter governments were continued without any change

Of course, there is a vital distinction between a government being dependent upon the will of the people or of the governing class, and a government dependent upon the will of the Crown; but to the average man in the street there was little or no consciousness that the government of his state after 1776 was in any way different from the government as it had been five or ten years before. Perhaps there was a feeling of contentment, because the government was his, but in the actual running of it there was little or no difference. On the one hand, this meant a continuation of the old order, with an aristocracy in control; while, on the other hand, forces were at work which were tending toward democracy. Property qualifications and other limitations upon both voting and office-holding were still the order of the day, but the requirements were lowered. Practically all of the incidents of feudal tenure disappeared. Primogeniture was abolished in aristocratic Virginia, and four of the states declared against the entailment of estates.

While these were all steps in the direction of democracy, they did not mean a sudden break with the past. Indeed, one of the best features of the Revolution was its being so little revolutionary or radical. The changes which it brought about were for the most part gradual and therefore more acceptable and more lasting. A shrewd English observer, the phrenologist, George Combe, traveling in the United States in 1840, wrote in his *Notes:* —

The generation of 1775 was trained under a monarchy, and they had the feelings and habits of Englishmen. When their independence was achieved, their mental condition was not instantly changed. Their deference for rank and for judicial and legislative authority, continued nearly unimpaired.

An appreciation of that fact is indispensable in understanding the course of American development.

The Confederation In addition to the local state governments some sort of a union and central organization was necessary, and the Congress made up of delegates from the various states which had come into existence in 1774 as a temporary expedient was continued and made permanent. Its composition was formally determined and its powers defined in the Articles of Confederation. But the Articles were not finally ratified and in operation until 1781, and in the meantime Congress went calmly on its way. To be sure, it was not an aggressive body, although it was the only central organ of government. But how could it be aggressive? It was made up of state delegations, all of which, large and small, were upon an equal footing. Nominally it was granted extensive powers, but none of the more important could be exercised without the consent of nine states, which was equivalent to requiring a two-thirds vote; and no sort of obedience could be enforced as there was merely a declaration in the Articles that "every State shall abide by the determinations of the United States in Congress assembled."

The "determinations" of Congress were therefore little better than recommendations, and this was deplorably shown in the matter of raising money. Congress had authority only to determine the amounts that were needed and to apportion to each state its share. The states honored those requisitions exactly to the extent that each saw fit; and Congress had no power and no right to enforce payment. Under such circumstances the financial difficulties of the government may readily be imagined. Unable to obtain the necessary amounts from the states, Congress borrowed from foreign governments where it could, and then resorted to the unfortunate expedient of issuing paper money in quantities.

From the vantage-point of the twentieth century, after long experience in popular government, it is customary to criticize the Confederation and condemn its organization as altogether unworkable. That is probably unfair, and it certainly does not represent the attitude or the opinion of the men of that time. The Confederation was the first essay in united government that the people of the newly independent states had made. No one claimed that it was perfect, but Jefferson probably expressed the attitude of his fellows when he wrote that "with all the imperfections of our present government, it is without comparison the best existing or that ever did exist." In another burst of enthusiasm Jefferson had said that a comparison of American government with the governments of Europe "is like a comparison of heaven and hell. England, like the earth, may be allowed to take the intermediate station."

Public lands The reason for the long delay in ratifying the Articles of Confederation was an uncertainty as to the ownership of the lands west of the Allegheny Mountains. Most of the desirable land east of the mountains had been taken up before the middle of the eighteenth century, and expansion farther to the west had first been checked by the Indians and then formally prohibited, as we have seen, by the Proclamation of 1763. Settlers, however, had been permitted to make their way into western Pennsylvania in the neighborhood of Pittsburgh, and they had also gone south of the Ohio River, into the region now known as Kentucky and Tennessee, in sufficient numbers to obtain recognition and to take an important though inconspicuous part in the fighting of the Revolution.

The Western country was therefore of practical and of immediate interest. Some states were claiming large parts of it by virtue of their colonial charter grants "from sea to sea."

Other states with fixed boundaries could put forward no such claims and, being limited in their expansion, were fearful lest they should be overwhelmed in the future by the more fortunate property-owning states. Accordingly they refused to ratify the plan of union unless the Western lands, or at least so much of them as were not already occupied, should be used for the benefit of the United States as a whole. Maryland and Delaware were particularly insistent upon this point and finally forced the claimants to yield. Beginning in 1780 one state after another ceded to Congress its claims to the territory north and west of the Ohio River, and the United States thereby came into the possession of a public domain estimated to amount to one or two hundred million acres, and supposed to be worth about a dollar an acre. This was an asset sufficient to meet the debt incurred in the war and to leave a balance for the running expenses of the Government.

When the Treaty of Peace, in 1783, determined that the country between the Alleghenies and the Mississippi was to belong to the United States and not to any foreign power, the pent-up population broke west of the mountains in a genuine flood. In 1779 it was said that there were only one hundred and seventy-six white men in the whole Kentucky dis-

trict; but by 1785 the population was estimated at from 20,000 to 30,000, and according
to the census of 1790 there were 73,000 in
Kentucky and 35,000 in Tennessee. The
United States property was northwest of the
Ohio River, and there was certain to be a
great demand for it as soon as it was opened
up. Congress, therefore, faced two important
Western problems demanding solution: one
was to determine the policy for disposing of
its public lands; and the other was to provide
a government for settlers upon those lands.

The answer to the first was found in the
Land Ordinance of 1785. As adopted by
Congress it provided for the rectangular survey
of the public domain into townships six miles
square, each of which was divided into thirty-
six sections, and the townships were to be sold,
alternately, as a whole and by sections, at
prices not less than one dollar an acre. The
financial aspect is predominant, for this meant
sale in large lots of over 20,000 acres and in
small lots of 640 acres; but the purpose of encouraging settlement was not lost sight of, and
it was prophetic of a most striking phase of
American development when this early law
contained a provision that the sixteenth section in each township was to be reserved for
the maintenance of public schools. The details
are tedious, but the mechanical rectangular

method of survey and the requirement that the land must be surveyed before it could be sold made possible a simple system of recording titles, rendered transfers of property easy, and thereby did away with endless confusion. It proved to be a simple and permanently excellent system which has been widely copied.

Coloni-zation The problem of government was referred to a committee of which Thomas Jefferson was chairman, where he rendered a service similar to his formulation of the Declaration of Independence, by taking up ideas that were current in the air and expressing them in an acceptable form. The people of the United States were accustomed to self-government, and in the process of expansion they had seen new colonies and even new states come into being. Vermont, although not yet recognized as a member of the Union, had declared itself to be an independent state and had a government of its own. Kentucky was practically independent of Virginia. The formation of new states was therefore not a new conception and, in the first proposals with reference to ceding the Western country to Congress, it was suggested that the territory ceded should be divided up into states. Upon the basis of these ideas Jefferson framed his Ordinance of 1784. There were features that were not satisfactory and it was never actually put into operation, yet it alone made possible its more famous successor.

In the summer of 1787 representatives of the Ohio Company, composed largely of New England Revolutionary veterans, came to Congress and proposed to purchase a million acres of Western land. In view of the size of the purchase, the price was reduced to two thirds of a dollar an acre. Part of this, at least, could be paid in Federal certificates of indebtedness, which were worth about twelve cents on the dollar, so that the actual price was reduced to eight or nine cents an acre. It seems to have been a part of the bargain that an ordinance of government satisfactory to the company should be adopted. Before the bargain could be completed the land sale was enlarged so as to grant a share in it to certain influential financial interests in New York, where Congress was sitting, and certain concessions were made to members of Congress. The additional land sale was for five million acres, on practically the same terms. Such was the sordid origin of the Ordinance of 1787, which "has been perhaps the most notable instance of legislation that was ever enacted by the representatives of the American people."

One clause of the ordinance prohibited slavery in the Northwest Territory, and owing to a combination of circumstances it has distracted attention from more important features, for the practical working of the government is the significant thing, as it was with the first state constitutions. Details are not essential; the ordinance provided for an increasing measure of self-government and ultimate admission into the Union on a footing of equality with the original states. Although differing in particulars, those were the fundamental principles of Jefferson's ordinance which were thus embodied in the Ordinance of 1787.

The new states that were thus planned for the West were in reality colonies, but American experience attached an unfortunate stigma to that word, and so the "territory" northwest of the Ohio River grew to be the generic name. As each new territory was formed, the Ordinance of 1787 was extended over it, and while in the course of one hundred and thirty years some provisions have been modified and details have been changed, the principles of the territorial system have remained the same. The unique feature of the system is the incorporation of the colony into the parent state, and not only has it proved to be most successful, it also has made this one of the best colonial systems the world has known. The United States at the present time consists of forty-eight separate states. Aside from the original thirteen, only six states have come into the Union without having been territories, and four of these six had had an equivalent training. The remaining twenty-nine have all passed through the territorial stage. The experience in self-government thus acquired, an experience wisely ordered to be under a form of government modeled on that of the original states and already found to be good, has led the people of a territory, in every instance, when allowed to form their own state government, to follow the model which had been set for them. Similarity of training and experience explains the fact, so often the subject of comment, that all of the states in the Union at the present time are so much alike in their form of government.

A consideration of even larger significance is that, if such a process of incorporation is continued long enough, the colonies will become greater than the mother country and the colonists will outnumber the parent stock. This has been the case in the United States. The three or four million people reported by the Census of 1790 have become the hundred million of the present, nearly seventy per cent of whom live beyond the Allegheny Mountains. The colonists of 1787 have grown into the American people of to-day.

Foreign trade

In separating from Great Britain the Americans seem never to have realized the full consequences of their act. As colonists they had been inclined to make much more of the restrictions that were placed upon them than of the benefits they enjoyed under British rule, and they apparently thought that with independence they would be free to trade where they pleased. As a matter of fact they found themselves outside of the Empire and automatically excluded from sharing in British colonial commerce. To make matters worse, when peace came, France annulled decrees which had given peculiar privileges to Americans, and Spain closed many of her ports to their shipping. Although there had been some necessary development of manufactures during the Revolution, the Americans were still engaged mainly in agriculture and other extractive industries, so that they were in the same dependent stage as formerly, where they had to rely upon outside markets. So far as trade was concerned the Americans independent were worse off than they had been under the British system.

If it is recalled how important the West India trade was in colonial economy, it will be seen why the reopening of that trade was regarded as essential to the prosperity of the United States.

There seemed to be but one way by which former commercial privileges could be restored, and that was through retaliatory measures, which Congress had no power to take. Accordingly, various amendments to the Articles of Confederation were proposed for the purposes of providing increased revenue and of giving to Congress power over commerce, but all of these proposals failed because amendments required the unanimous consent of the states and this could not be secured.

With that wonderful adaptability which was becoming characteristic of them the Americans were adjusting themselves to the new conditions. They were practicing economy after the speculation and extravagance of war times; they were trying further to develop their manufactures; and they were seeking out new channels of trade, as to the East Indies. It helped greatly that France was soon obliged to modify the enforcement of her colonial policy, and that Spain relaxed her restrictions, and that even the British made concessions. But while the situation was improving, several years elapsed before conditions were restored to anything like what they had been preceding the break with Great Britain, and, as is usually the case, it took a long time for the slowly recovering prosperity to be generally appreciated. In the meantime Americans were greatly dissatisfied, and hard times in 1784 and 1785 made them still more impatient.

Apparently there was no doubt in their minds as to what was the trouble, for without contradiction it was officially asserted that "Commerce . . . is the constant source of wealth and incentive to industry; and the value of our produce and our land must ever rise or fall in proportion to the prosperity or adverse state of trade." It was in the endeavor to remedy the situation that delegates from the several states were invited to meet in convention at Annapolis in 1786 to "take into consideration the trade of the United States." When only a few attended, it seemed advisable to do nothing beyond recommending another convention the next year in Philadelphia to attack the larger problem of revising the Articles of Confederation so as to render them "adequate to the exigencies of the union."

The Federal Convention
So far this had been a voluntary effort or a self-imposed task, but when authorized by Congress and approved by the states it grew into the Federal Convention of 1787. This was a small body of fifty-five at the most, and with scarcely more than thirty ordinarily in attendance, but it included some of the best-known men in the United States. When Jefferson heard of the first appointments, he wrote from

Paris, "It really is an assembly of demi-gods." That may have been true of some delegates, but with these greater men there were also men of less importance and of lesser ability. There were politicians as well as statesmen, and there were some who were quite unfit for the task as well as some who were trained by experience and study. As a whole it was a fairly representative gathering, but because it was made up almost entirely from men of the upper class, and because of the character of its leaders, it was possibly of a little better type and of a little higher tone than would be a similar body at the present time.

Although George Washington was the most distinguished, and in a way the most important, member of the convention, as was shown by his unanimous selection to be the presiding officer, the greatest credit for what was done belongs to James Madison, of Virginia. His was apparently the master mind preparing the plan and shaping the work, though of course accepting many modifications, which were suggested and sometimes forced upon him by others. He was supported throughout by Washington and had the active assistance on the floor of Governor Edmund Randolph and of most of the other members of the Virginia delegation, and of such men as James Wilson and Gouverneur Morris of Pennsylvania, General Charles Cotesworth

Pinckney and John Rutledge of South Carolina, and Rufus King of Massachusetts.

The convention had been called to amend the Articles of Confederation, but when thoughtful members began to consider the defects which would have to be remedied, these proved to be so numerous that the far-sighted were convinced that a complete change in the organization of government was necessary. It is doubtful whether a majority of the delegates had ever considered such a contingency or would have approved of such radical action if they had. And so the supporters of a new form of government had to move carefully, in order not to antagonize but to win over a sufficient number to the support of their cause.

The real difference between the two opinions in the convention was whether the legislative power should be vested in a congress chosen in proportion to population or in a congress which should be, as in the Confederation, representative of the states. It was an issue between the large and small states, but it was also an issue between an effective national government and the old ineffective league of states. So evenly were the forces divided that it meant a disruption of the convention unless an adjustment could be made. After weeks of bitter discussion a compromise was agreed to by which the lower house of Congress was to be composed of representatives elected from the various states in proportion to the numbers of population, in which only three fifths of the slaves were to be counted, and the upper house was to consist of two senators from each state.

Once this compromise was reached and the small states mollified by obtaining equal representation in one house, the work proceeded much more smoothly and easily, although further compromises were necessary at every step. To the legislature when established powers were given greater than those of the Confederation, especially in matters of taxation and commerce, but the all-important feature was in making it possible for the central government to enforce its will. Congress was authorized "to provide for calling forth the Militia to execute the Laws of the Union," while more significant still was a declaration in the final article that "This Constitution . . . shall be the supreme Law of the Land." Not a treaty, nor an agreement between states, but a law enacted by the highest of all lawmaking bodies, the people; and though its enforcement was backed by the armed power of the Nation, as a law it was enforceable in the courts.

Although not nearly so disrupting as had been the question of representation, the most difficult problem which the convention had to solve was connected with the executive. The men of that day could think only in terms of monarchy, and as Americans wanted an official with royal power who would not be a king, the method of choice and tenure of office were the all-important considerations. After seemingly endless discussions and hopeless confusion, the opinion of the majority finally emerged in favor of a short term of four years, with eligibility to reëlection. They thought that the executive must be independent of the legislature, so he should not be chosen by it; and as they were afraid of a popular election, they finally compromised upon a scheme which it is said came indirectly from the Papal College. There was to be a college of electors composed of members chosen by the legislature of each state, and each elector was to be free to vote for whom he pleased. No person could be chosen President who did not receive a majority of the electoral votes, but as there was to be no meeting of the electors, which would permit canvassing and reaching an agreement, it was expected that in the great majority of cases no election would result, and it was then provided that Congress should choose the President from the five men who had received the largest number of votes. Not foreseeing the concentration of votes made possible through political party organization, it was expected that the method adopted would probably result in the electoral college

CHAPTER IV

THE NEW GOVERNMENT

REASONS have been given for the success of the Constitution and of the new Government, but in the inauguration of the latter great credit should also be ascribed to George Washington. As was expected, and as had been intimated even in the Federal Convention when the office of the executive was under discussion, there was no difference of opinion among the electors, and by their unanimous vote Washington became the first President of the United States. One indication of Washington's greatness was his willingness to recognize and to use the superior ability of others. He accordingly chose able advisers, chief among whom were Thomas Jefferson as Secretary of State, and Alexander Hamilton as Secretary of the Treasury. While the former, by virtue of his position, was in a sense the leading member of the Administration, the work of Hamilton, in view of conditions, was more immediately important.

Finance The most pressing needs of the Government were financial, and the first measure passed by Congress, after a formal enactment providing for the taking of the oaths of office, was a revenue act levying moderate duties upon imports. At the same time a tonnage act was adopted imposing duties upon shipping, and this was also in the nature of a navigation act, for by discriminating duties it encouraged American shipping at the expense of foreign, and forced the coastwise trade into American vessels. These acts were important, but the real financial problem was a larger one and was left for Hamilton to solve. His successful handling of it stands out conspicuously, even in a career that was otherwise brilliant. The establishment of the credit of the United States was the object which he sought to attain, and his recommendations thereto were presented in a series of masterly reports. His chief proposals were: the funding or bonding of the United States debt, both foreign and domestic, so as to place all forms of it on a uniform stable basis; the assumption by the Federal Government of the war debts incurred by the individual states; increased taxation to provide the additional revenue necessary; and the establishment of a central financial institution in the form of a national bank.

This was going farther than most people had cou ted on and aroused considerable opposition, some of which was temperamental, and some was justifiable. It meant an unexpected and perhaps unwarranted exercise of power by the central government, arousing the fears of many good citizens; and there was also not a little speculation in Government securities, leading to the cry of "Favored interests!" which would profit by the rise in values. It took some manipulation, therefore, such as winning the support of Southern members by yielding to them the location of the national capital on the Potomac, and some slight concessions had to be made, but the Secretary finally succeeded in getting his proposals through Congress substantially in the form in which they had been presented.

Like most large schemes, Hamilton's financial undertakings involved an element of risk. This was not because they were beyond the resources of the United States, but because they went beyond the willingness of the people to carry the burden. The country was experiencing, as it had in the days of the Confederation, some of the unfortunate consequences of things done in Revolutionary times. The people were so unaccustomed that they were really opposed to taxation, and their antipathy proved to be so deep and lasting that the United States, beginning in 1789, grew more and more to depend upon indirect taxation, which is not so immediately felt. One of Hamilton's reasons for insisting upon an excise tax was that the people might be taught to accept taxation, and he was not unwilling to assume the responsibility of putting down opposition, as proved to be necessary in the so-called Whiskey Insurrection in Pennsylvania in 1794.

Even with the increases in tariff rates that were made, and taking into account all other sources of income, the fact remains that the revenues were insufficient to meet the growing expenses of the Government and of the funded debt as well. Unless the people were willing to make much greater sacrifices than they ever had made in the past or had shown any disposition to make, there was a prospect that Hamilton's financial plans would have ended in partial failure at least. The crisis did not come, because the situation was relieved by help from an entirely unlooked-for source.

Foreign relations With the establishment of peace in 1783 the United States had sunk into insignificance, for there is no mistaking the attitude and actions of other nations. Spain, still hopeful of obtaining the region south and west of the Ohio River, alternately intrigued with the Indians and plotted with discontented Americans, in fine disregard of the Government of the United States. In the Northwest the British retained military posts contrary to treaty stipulations, although there was some justification or excuse in the claim that the Americans had failed to live up to their side of the agreement. The humiliating thing was that the Americans might object and protest but they could not prevent the retention of these forts within their own boundaries. The light in which the British regarded their former colonies is shown by their refusal to commission a minister to the United States for nearly ten years. Even France treated the United States as a protégé and not as an equal. The heart of the whole matter is found in an assertion by Captain Isaac Snow of Harpswell, when the Federal Constitution was under consideration in Massachusetts: "I, sir, since the war, have had commerce with six different nations of the globe, and . . . I find this country held in the same light by foreign nations, as a well-behaved negro in a gentleman's family."

When war broke out in Europe in 1793, the United States again rose to a position of some consequence. The people were following the course of the French Revolution with eager interest. The abolition of the monarchy received general approval. The proclamation of the Convention declaring it to be the mission of France to establish the liberty of peoples against kings met with marked sympathy, and when told that this meant carrying the gospel of American liberty to all the world their enthusiasm was unrestrained. There was an extraordinary series of celebrations in all parts of the United States, such as banquets, civic feasts, and processions, accompanied with bonfires, bell-ringing, and the firing of cannon. Democratic societies were formed, and one at least, in Charleston, was actually adopted by the Jacobin Club of Paris. As a further indication of sympathy and approval titles were declared to be absurd in a republic and some who opposed even the use of "Mr." addressed each other as "Citizen." When Genêt, the minister of the French Republic, arrived in the United States the reception accorded to him was in the nature of an ovation.

But the execution of Louis XVI, followed as it was by the war with Great Britain, Holland, and Spain, made Americans hesitate and consider, and so when Washington issued a proclamation declaring that the United States would maintain "a conduct friendly and impartial towards the belligerent powers," it came as a dash of cold water to bring them to their senses. Washington's Proclamation, and an act of Congress in the following year enforcing it, set a new standard of neutrality in international law. From the standpoint of the development of the United States the action was undoubtedly justifiable, for it was important that the country should be kept out of European quarrels and should be free to work out its own salvation. Accordingly reasons were found for refusing to accept any obligation under the treaties of 1778, yet the fact cannot be ignored that, in view of what the French had done for the United States in its war for independence, Americans have been on the defensive with regard to this neutrality.

Neutral trade To those who have seen the enormous profits going to neutrals in the Great War, it is not necessary to explain the advantages accruing from neutrality. The details may have been different, but the essentials were the same in 1793 as in 1914. With the outbreak of war France immediately threw open her colonial ports to neutrals, and the Americans, by their geographic position, and having not only the best of ships and sailors, but also surplus products in abundance, were ready and eager to take advantage of the situation. The French quickly appreciated the benefit of this to them and were in a measure reconciled to American neutrality. But Great Britain could not sit idly by and let her enemy be relieved from the pressure which she ought to have been able to exert by her superior navy. Upon the assertion of principles, such as the so-called Rule of 1756, and by an extension of the list of contraband, she began seizing American vessels in the West Indies. Relations were strained to the breaking point, but Great Britain could not afford to antagonize the United States by too drastic measures. Jay's Treaty of 1794 removed some of the most serious causes of difficulty and arranged for the settlement of others, and as is usual in such cases a *modus operandi* was developed. The demand in Europe was for West Indian products. The Americans had a perfect right to trade directly with the belligerent countries, provided it was in articles not contraband of war. They might also trade directly with the European colonies in the West Indies. Accordingly goods were transported from the West Indies to the United States, where they were landed and duties upon them were paid; they thereby became a part of the stock of the United States, and could then be carried to Europe.

Apparently the British acquiesced in this in the belief that, because of the expense and amount of capital required, the indirect trade could not be carried on to such an extent as to do any great harm. Yet the trade grew by leaps and bounds. At the present day we are so accustomed to dealing in billions that the figures of the eighteenth and early nineteenth centuries seem pitiably small. But proportions may indicate what this meant to the United States. In the course of a few years the tonnage of American vessels engaged in the neutral trade more than doubled, while exports increased to five times their previous amounts, and the larger share of these exports represented the products of foreign countries.

The profits of the carrying trade were accordingly large, and yet a relatively small class was affected in comparison with those who were benefited by the increased demand for American articles. The West India islands, as of old, wanted foodstuffs and lumber; while the feeding of the immense armies called for American assistance, all the greater because of the shortage of crops in Europe; and military needs still further enlarged the demand for lumber from the United States. Under these conditions the exports of domestic products from the United States more than doubled, and prices were affected to almost the same extent. For example, the average price for flour for several years before 1793 had been $5.40 a barrel, and the average for twelve years thereafter was $9.12, an increase of about seventy per cent. So great were the profits from this commodity that Virginia was led into grain-raising on an extensive scale and, in the country west of the Alleghenies, Kentucky and Tennessee became flour-exporting states.

The neutral trade was the unexpected factor that came to the rescue of Hamilton's financial plans. It meant more than ordinary prosperity; it brought comparatively great wealth, and it seems to have been responsible for the accumulation of a surplus fund of capital for the first time in fairly large quantities. The increased revenues of the Government, directly and indirectly from the neutral trade, made it possible to meet all running expenses, to pay the interest on the debt, and to take up bonds as they became due. It is evident at once that the neutral trade of 1793 corresponded closely to the old trade of colonial days. There were differences, of course; the demand for certain products fell off, while that for others increased; and a new Southern export was found in cotton, which, with the invention of the cotton gin, became an increasingly important item. The underlying features of the trade, however, remained the same, the fundamental principle being that the people of the United States were still relying upon their extractive industries and were still dependent upon foreign markets and foreign manufactures.

Political parties Developments, such as have been described as taking place in the United States, inevitably caused divisions in public opinion; not even the Revolution had been fought by a united people. But although British parties had been reproduced in America, with the Whigs as patriots and the Tories thereby becoming a name of reproach, this did not mean that there was any fundamental political organization, and when the war was over only Whigs remained. Of course, local politics had always aroused differences of opinion and consequently factions and local organizations had developed. The ground was therefore ready and no sooner was there a national development, with questions of national scope arising, than divisions of opinion on a nation-wide scale were evident and political parties representative of them grew up.

The ratification of the Constitution presented such a question, with the Federalists supporting the new form of government and the Anti-Federalists opposing it. When the decision was in favor of adoption the great majority of the people in the United States, even of the opposition, believed in supporting the new Government and giving it an opportunity to try itself out. And so the Anti-Federalists disappeared, but the differences of opinion did not, for they represented a diversity as old as mankind between the conservative and the radical. On this occasion the variance was between those who were in favor of a strongly centralized government and those who preferred decentralization of power. It was also a difference between those who believed in the control of affairs by the select few, or by the upper class, and those who believed in advancing the interests of the mass of the people.

A divergence so fundamental was certain again to manifest itself as soon as a sufficiently important question arose, and that occurred almost immediately in connection with the measures relating to finance. All were agreed on the necessity of a revenue, but there was no agreement as to the ways and means of raising it. An aggressive policy like Hamilton's was bound to arouse opposition. That was only human. Men who were in hearty sympathy with his object differed with him as to methods. Antagonism that was more serious came from a personal distrust of him and his supporters. The inevitable speculation in Government securities had greatly profited certain individuals, and it was believed that this was due not merely to foresight but to the advantage of inside information. Accordingly there developed a strong opposition to paying the full value of Government securities to the present holders rather than to the original owners. There also arose a sharp divergence as to the justice or injustice of the assumption of the state debts; and there was a further radical difference of opinion on the advisability of an excise tax. Each of these measures in turn tended to strengthen the opposition until the climax was reached on the question of a national bank.

Such consistent divisions as have been noted

are apt to find their justification in some more fundamental principle than that of mere policy. Inasmuch as the Government of the United States was organized under a written constitution it was natural that the differences of opinion should ultimately turn upon the interpretation of that document, — that is, as to whether the measures proposed were permissible or not under the fundamental instrument of government. With a strict interpretation of the Constitution it did not seem that a central national bank could be justified, however desirable it might be. By the very circumstances of the case the opponents of the Administration were forced into being strict constructionists.

Like every other human activity there is always a personal element in the organization of a political party which needs to be taken into account; and while motives are not easy to determine, leadership usually stands out clear and recognizable. By temperament as well as by fate Hamilton was designated as the leader of the Administration and its supporters, who seized the prestige coming from the adoption of the Constitution and called themselves Federalists. They represented the continuance of the established order and the maintenance in control of affairs of the same ruling class that had dominated in colonial times.

89

Into the new opposition there went many of the former Anti-Federalists; it was natural that those who had been opposed to the Constitution should now be in favor of the strictest limitation of that document. Madison, however, had been a loyal supporter of the Constitution, and yet he was one of the prominent men in the new party. It is evident, then, that the party represented something more than strict construction, and in fact it contained the radical and more democratic elements of the community. These men liked to call themselves Republicans, but the Federalists also called themselves Republicans, and so a convenient name for the party of the opposition became that of Democratic-Republicans. They found their natural leader in Thomas Jefferson.

The rest of the party development followed in the ordinary course of events. Washington might advise his fellow citizens strongly against the danger of "cabal," and he might try to keep aloof from partisan prejudices, but from temperament as well as from acceptance and support of Hamilton's ideas he became a Federalist in spite of himself. While his appointments were made mainly on the basis of ability and fitness, instances were increasing in which it was necessary or advisable to have men who were friendly to the Administration. It was found more convenient for his chief executive officers to meet together with him for consultation and so form what is called the Cabinet, and it seemed impossible to have such a body of advisers with opinions radically in opposition to one another. There was only one outcome, and that was the appointment of the chief executive officers and then of most other officers from men of one party.

There is little doubt that the Federalists represented what had always been a minority of the population, and it was not alone the limitations of the suffrage that prevented the majority from gaining control; custom and social deference had much to do with it. The first service which Jefferson and the Democratic-Republican party are said to have rendered was in persuading the ordinary man that he had a right to vote against the wishes of his so-called superiors. But it was also a matter of ignorance and indifference, for most men did not know and did not care about political questions until, by propaganda and an organized system of committees, the Democratic-Republicans aroused them and succeeded, as we should say, in "getting out the vote." Federalists of the old order protested against such organization and methods, not as being unconstitutional, but as being extra-legal, as contrary to the established order, and they even went so far as to intimate and occasionally openly to charge that such action was treasonable. Yet protests were of no avail against the rising strength of democracy, except that they may have held it in restraint for a few years.

Foreign relations To the present generation of Americans it seems unnecessary, but Washington knew his countrymen and their faults when he inserted in his Farewell Address the warning against "passionate attachment" to any other nation, for oddly enough, after the subject of finance, about the most important division in domestic politics was on questions of foreign relations. By social as well as by financial connections, that is as a class, the Federalists were closely in touch with the British and, as a matter of course, in sympathy with them. Indeed, it might fairly be said of official America that its neutrality was friendly to Great Britain. Party antagonism therefore as well as natural inclination led the Democratic-Republicans to become pro-French and to favor the French Revolution. To show how far they were carried by their feelings, John Davis noted in his *Travels* that shortly after his arrival in the United States in 1798, having translated for Caritat, the bookseller, *Campaigns of Buonaparte in Italy*, "on the fourth of June it was ushered into the literary world amidst the acclamations of the Democrats, and the revilings of the Federalists. This was to me extraordinary."

The foreign situation was so complicated that it is little wonder that Americans were bewildered and that at times the political parties were inconsistent in their attitude. Jay's Treaty had removed the immediate danger of trouble between Great Britain and the United States, and after France and Spain came together in the Peace of Basle in 1795, it seemed as if it produced opposite effects upon these two countries. Spain was evidently expecting that trouble would result and thought that there was no use in adding the United States to her enemies, and accordingly sought to obtain merit by yielding on all the points at issue with that country. The disputed boundary question in the Southwest was settled in accordance with American claims, and not only was the free navigation of the Mississippi River recognized, but the all-important right of deposit at New Orleans was granted to the Americans. In fact, it was this treaty of San Lorenzo which made it possible for the West to share in the neutral trade. On the other hand, with each successive triumph of France in the European struggle the United States became of less and less importance to her and she was pleased to regard Jay's Treaty as evincing an unfriendly disposition. However, France was not yet ready for an open breach, and some conciliatory efforts were made with an eye to the election of 1796, for party attitudes were well known and much was hoped from the man who might succeed Washington in the presidency. When the Federalists were successful in electing John Adams it seems as if the French did not consider it worth while to try any more, and relations between the two countries rapidly went from bad to worse. Representatives were recalled, treaties were suspended, commercial intercourse was stopped, and active preparations for war were made. Although ships were seized and conflicts occurred between armed vessels of the two countries, war was never formally declared, for France did not want war with the United States, and just when the outlook seemed darkest overtures were made which rendered possible the restoration of Americans to their former position of neutrality. With Napoleon rising into power, a convention was concluded in 1800 which disposed of former treaties and established a satisfactory working basis. So near to war had it come, however, that later, when passing upon claims for damages, the Supreme Court of the United States declared that "virtual warfare" had existed in 1798.

Domestic politics When the crisis became acute party differences were allowed to disappear, the Democratic-Republicans showed that they were first of all Americans, and the whole country became anti-French. The Federalists wisely made use of this unanimity in pressing active measures preparatory to war; but they used it unwisely in trying to obtain political advantages. There were many foreigners in the United States who had been more or less a source of trouble and who certainly were thorns in the side of the Administration. Moreover, the Democratic-Republicans had quickly appreciated the advantage of the press and in a quite modern way had even founded newspapers for the spread of their ideas, while the language used was of such a character that modern newspaper vituperation seems mild in comparison. In other words the situation may have warranted some action on the part of the Government, but in the passing of four acts commonly known as the Alien and Sedition Acts, in 1798, the Federalists went too far. They not only made naturalization too difficult, but they also placed arbitrary powers in the hands of the Government, and they established what were regarded as limitations on the freedom of the press. Their methods may have been constitutional; there is little doubt that they were inexpedient.

The Democratic-Republicans in their turn were also jockeying for a position of political advantage. In a series of resolutions which, because they were adopted by the legislatures of those states, became known as the Kentucky and Virginia Resolutions of 1798 and 1799, Jefferson and Madison laid down certain general principles declaring the Constitution to be a compact to which the states were parties and, when the Federal Government overstepped the powers therein granted, that the states should be the judges both of the infraction and of the mode of redress. While the resolutions never accomplished much practically, they remained as a political platform of the Democratic-Republicans in particular, but also in general as a statement of principles for any party out of power.

The day of the Federalists was evidently passing, but it was the combination of events that brought about their downfall. They overreached themselves in the Alien and Sedition Acts and that may well have been the finishing touch, or it may have been the death of Washington in 1799, for his name and support had always been their greatest asset. The Democratic-Republicans had been sufficiently strong to obtain the second largest vote for Thomas Jefferson in 1796, thereby making him Vice-President, and in 1800 they were successful in electing him to the presidency.

BIBLIOGRAPHY

Besides the general histories already noticed, special mention should be made of James Schouler, *History of the United States under the Constitution* (7 vols., 1880–1913). J. S. Bassett, *The Federalist System* (1906), is limited to the administrations of Washington and Adams. C. R. Fish, *American Diplomacy* (1915), contains the best account of the foreign relations of the United States, but without appreciating the full significance of the neutral carrying trade.

Among the many special studies, the subjects of which are indicated by their titles, attention should be called to H. J. Ford, *Rise and Growth of American Politics: a Sketch of Constitutional Development* (1898); M. Ostrogorski, *Democracy and the Party System in the United States, a Study in Extra-Constitutional Government* (1910); H. B. Learned, *The President's Cabinet* (1912); C. R. Fish, *The Civil Service and the Patronage* (1905); D. R. Dewey, *Financial History of the United States* (1903); C. A. Beard, *Economic Origins of Jeffersonian Democracy* (1915).

Biographies are so numerous that to mention any of them is only to invite the charge of discrimination, but most of the volumes in the *American Statesman* series (1882–1900), edited by J. T. Morse, Jr., are well worth reading. Among the best of the others are W. C. Ford, *George Washington* (2 vols., 1900); W. G. Sumner, *Alexander Hamilton* (1890); F. S. Oliver, *Alexander Hamilton, an Essay on American Union* (1907).

CHAPTER V

LIBERAL GOVERNMENT

THE success of the popular party in the election of Jefferson was often referred to as " the Revolution of 1800." The changes brought about were indeed far-reaching, but proved to be rather different in character from what had been expected. On the one hand, the disaster freely predicted by the gloomy Federalists did not materialize; in fact, the country prospered under a Republican régime. On the other hand, the Democratic-Republicans failed to redeem their promises to undo as much as possible of the mischief that had been wrought by the Federalists. They started out bravely enough by repealing legislation and removing objectionable officials; but, having been elected upon principles of economy and a stricter construction of the Constitution, they were compelled in a short time by the very force of circumstances to repudiate their own doctrines and to adopt those of their opponents, as well as to follow their opponents' way of doing things.

The Old National Road As has been so frequently the case expansion was a large element in the new phases of American development. By 1800 the population of the

Northwest had increased to such an extent that a division of the territory became advisable, in preparation for the admission of the eastern part into the Union as a state. This new state of Ohio, the first child of the territorial system, afforded an excuse for the building of a better road from east to west by the National Government. There was no constitutional authority for spending the public money for such a purpose, but on the basis of a *quid pro quo* of exemption from taxation, it was agreed to devote a certain percentage of the proceeds of public land sales in Ohio for this purpose. When the amounts were insufficient Congress, in the form of "advances," supplied additional funds to several times the amount that could ever be received in return. The same practice was followed with each of the other new states in turn as it was admitted into the Union, so that the road was extended to the Mississippi River and beyond. But Congress grew tired of this pretense, as well as of paying for repairs and maintenance, and eventually the road was given by the Federal Government to the states through which it passed. The formalities had been observed, but the Old National Road had been built at Government expense and under the sanction of a strict construction party.

Louisiana Great as had been the increase of settlers in the Northwest, it was insignificant in comparison with the increase of population south of the Ohio; and together there were over 600,000 settlers west of the Alleghenies by 1800. For these people the question of transportation was vital. The Old National Road when completed would be useful, but it could by no means meet the growing needs of the West; the navigation of the Mississippi River was a practical necessity. The treaty with Spain in 1795 had relieved the situation temporarily, but it seemed as if Spain had not relinquished her hopes of some time owning or controlling what was left of the Southwest and she was following a policy not altogether friendly to the Americans. The privileges which she had granted by the treaty had in a way been wrested from her by the European situation.

An essential part of the navigation of the Mississippi was the right of deposit at the mouth of the river. This meant permission to land and transship goods without the payment of unduly heavy charges or duties. The first grant of this privilege had been for three years, and when that time expired, in 1798, Spain withdrew the right until a protest from the United States and a demonstration of force on the part of the Western settlers themselves led her to concede it again. The situation was a delicate one, requiring careful handling, but was apparently working out fairly satisfactorily for the United States, when suddenly the whole aspect was changed by the retrocession of Louisiana to France.

Dreaming apparently of the restoration not only of her old boundaries in Europe but of her former trans-Atlantic possessions, France again planned a colonial empire. With Napoleon in power it was easy to bring such pressure to bear as to induce Spain to give back the territory of Louisiana to France, which was done in 1802. The agreement was a secret one, but it had been generally understood in Europe long before and rumors of it had reached America, so that the Government was prepared to act. Just at this moment Spain once more withdrew the right of deposit. Jefferson at once wrote to the American representative in Paris, for the benefit of the French authorities, that it was a very different thing to have France instead of Spain in control of the mouth of the Mississippi River, — a strong nation instead of a weak one. Then he significantly added· "The day that France takes possession of New Orleans . . . seals the union of two nations, which in conjunction can maintain exclusive possession of the ocean. From that moment we must marry ourselves to the British fleet and nation."

Robert R. Livingston was the American minister to France; James Monroe was sent to join him; and they were authorized to offer ten million dollars for the possession of West Florida and New Orleans, so that the United States might own sufficient land at the mouth of the river to prevent any further disputes. What followed has always been one of the romantic, almost incredible incidents in American history. Whether Napoleon was tired of the colonial scheme, whether its difficulties discouraged him, whether it was on account of the inevitable resumption of the war with England, or whether it was because of a shortage of funds, will probably never be satisfactorily determined; perhaps all of them were elements in a complex situation. Jefferson's attitude must also have been a potent force: the friend of the French Revolution, strongly pro-French in sympathy, on being elected to the presidency had proved to be wholeheartedly American when the interests of his country were at stake. Napoleon's reasons may not have been clear, but there was no misunderstanding his proposal, when he suggested that instead of a comparatively small piece the United States should purchase the whole of Louisiana. The offer came as a surprise, but the American commissioners, seeing the opportunity, were wise enough and courageous enough to seize it. The terms were merely a matter of bargaining, and the total amount paid, including certain claims that were assumed by the United States, was $15,000,000.

However bold as a thinker, Jefferson was often hesitant in action, and he did not believe that it was within the power of the National Government to make this purchase. The size of Louisiana seemed to stagger him, for close reasoning must have shown him that if the United States could add on West Florida and New Orleans it could also acquire a larger area. But he could not reconcile it with his conscience, and he suggested an amendment to the Constitution which would authorize the purchase. Warned that there was no time for such delay lest Napoleon should change his mind, Jefferson reluctantly consented to allow the bargain to be completed, with the understanding that a constitutional amendment justifying the act should be subsequently adopted. To his surprise this was found to be unnecessary, for the purchase of Louisiana proved to be popular in the United States, and popular approval is a wonderful salve for a wounded political conscience. Strict construction of the Constitution meant something different after 1803 from what it had meant before.

The acquisition of Louisiana, like the Declaration of Independence, and the Ordinance of 1787, and the Federal Constitution, was an epoch-making event in American history. In the first place, it doubled the area of the United States, thereby increasing enormously the natural resources of the country. Then, too, like every other annexation of territory, it resulted in increasing the power of the central government; for in carrying out the provisions of the treaty, in the later sale of land, in the encouragement of settlement, and in the government of the territories that were formed, there was an exercise and inevitable strengthening of national authority. Finally, to mention nothing more, the mere control of the Mississippi River from its source to its mouth quieted discontent in the West and raised the Westerners' opinion of the government that could accomplish so much, and an excellent indication of this is the failure of Burr's Conspiracy a few years later. Whatever may have been the object of that expedition, it had relied upon the discontent of the West, and it failed when that was found to be lacking. The substance of the whole matter is that the acquisition of Louisiana resulted in a great strengthening of national feeling.

Barbary pirates One other matter in foreign relations brought great credit to Jefferson and his administration, and that was the war with Tripoli. Ever since his Paris days Jefferson had believed in the use of force rather than bribery in dealing with the Barbary pirates. So when he was elected to the presidency, in spite of the embarrassment to his Republican principles caused by the increased expense and the maintenance of a navy, Jefferson had insisted upon fighting against Tripoli. He conducted the war with energy and decision and brought it to a successful conclusion.

Neutral rights On the whole the Democratic-Republican Administration had been so great a success that in 1804 Jefferson was reëlected President with relatively little opposition. The brightness of his record, however, was dimmed during his second term of office because of foreign complications in which he showed less judgment and determination than he had in the case of Tripoli, perhaps because he was treating with stronger powers. The Napoleonic Wars, interrupted by the so-called Peace of Amiens, had broken out again in 1803 with Great Britain as the leader and the mainstay of the coalition that had formed against France. It soon came to a life-and-death struggle between these powers, for Nelson's naval victory at Trafalgar in the autumn of 1805 made the British supreme upon the sea, but Austerlitz in December left Napoleon more than ever master of the Continent.

Under the circumstances, however, it was fighting at long range as neither power could strike a vital blow. When it thereupon became a question of trying to starve each other out, it was evident that Great Britain must use the strength of her navy and her control of the sea. The neutral trade was relieving the enemy from some of the pressure, and the change in the British attitude toward that trade was admirably shown in the title of a pamphlet by James Stephen which received wide circulation, *War in Disguise, or the Frauds of the Neutral Flags*. It was still more clearly revealed in the case of the Essex in 1805, when the Lords Commissioners of Appeals declared that although goods had been landed in America and duties paid, they were still destined for the enemy and therefore subject to confiscation. The British were going back of the face of the records to the intent of the shipper.

But this was not enough, and a British Order in Council of 1806 announced a blockade from the port of Brest to the river Elbe, although it attempted to make it effective only from Ostend to the Seine. It may seem absurd, but privateers were making such serious inroads upon British commerce that color was given to Napoleon's claim that he would starve the British into yielding. And so, a few months after the British Order of 1806, he retorted with the Berlin Decree, which declared the British Islands in a state of blockade and forbade any vessel coming from Great Britain or the British colonies to be received in French ports. The British in turn, in January and November, 1807, forbade all coastal trade between French ports, and then declared a blockade of all ports from which the British were excluded, although some concessions were made to neutrals if they traded through English ports and paid certain duties. At last Napoleon, by his Milan Decree in December, declared that any vessel which submitted to the British orders was thereby rendered subject to seizure by the French.

Freight rates had been so high and profit so great that previously it had been worth while for the Americans to run the risk of their vessels being captured, but this new French and British retaliatory policy meant the annihilation of their carrying trade. Americans might protest against paper blockades and claim that "free ships make free goods," but that was useless in the intensity of the struggle between Great Britain and Napoleon. Both belligerents were over-stepping the boundaries of neutral rights, and each justified its action on the ground of provocation by the other. Napoleon was the more flagrant but Great Britain the more obvious transgressor, because the British were supreme upon the sea. Still the French could and did seize large numbers of American vessels in their ports. A most surprising, and to Americans humiliating, aspect of the situation was the way in which vessels of the belligerents patrolled the American coast and violated American neutrality. The French were as bad as the British except that their opportunities were more limited and so their acts were fewer, and the Americans would have been justified at almost any time during these years in going to war with either France or Great Britain.

A situation already difficult was rendered critical by the question of impressment, which hardly arose with the French at all, but with the British was at times so serious and always so dramatic as to supersede in the popular mind the more fundamental trouble of interference with the carrying trade. The British had always had hard work in maintaining the necessary number of men in their navy, and had been accustomed to rely upon enforced service or impressment. Even in colonial days the better wages and treatment in the American merchant service had attracted many English seamen, and now the demands of the neutral trade made it worth while for American shippers to offer still greater inducements, so that desertions from the British service were common.

As if this were not enough the matter was

further complicated by the opposing points of view on the subject of naturalization. The Americans being a nation of immigrants had found it necessary to their very existence that subjects of foreign powers should be allowed to become citizens of their state, and naturalization was one of the things early provided for. European powers had never been willing to recognize the principle of expatriation, and the British doctrine "once an Englishman always an Englishman" was the accepted standard. The British were right from their point of view, the Americans were right from theirs, and the matter could be settled only by international agreement which had not yet been reached. Furthermore, as there was no definition of United States citizenship and no clear distinction between that and citizenship of an individual state, each state was free to determine the conditions by which a person might become a citizen, and those terms were relatively easy, varying from a few months to a few years of residence. Under such circumstances naturalization papers were easily obtained, and many stories are current of the prices at which they were sold. The amount of it was that a deserter from a British vessel could quickly and cheaply obtain the necessary citizenship papers in the United States.

Enough has been said to show the unlimited

possibilities of trouble that existed, and it is aside from the mark to discuss the justice or injustice of impressment. If it ever had been right, it was justifiable at this time in the extremity of Great Britain's need. Yet that was after all a matter of British domestic policy; the Americans could only object to the way in which it was carried out. Even if Great Britain was warranted in stopping American vessels on the high seas and in searching for contraband, had she any right to search for deserters? Was an Englishman who had become an American citizen subject to impressment? These were in a sense idle questions; the British had the power and they were using it.

Whatever justification there may have been for what the British were doing, there was no excuse for the high-handed way in which they did it, and the only explanation is to be found in the passiveness of the Americans. The culmination was the unfortunate encounter in June, 1807, when the United States frigate Chesapeake was stopped outside of American territorial limits by the Leopard with a demand for deserters from certain specified British ships. Their existence on board being denied and right to search refused, the Chesapeake, unprepared, was fired upon and twenty-one men had been killed or wounded before one gun was at last discharged in return and the flag hauled down. The order for search was then carried out and four men were taken as deserters. The extent of the outrage may be gauged by the fact that of the four one was hanged, one died, and the other two, after five years of bitter wrangling, were restored to the deck of the Chesapeake, and the American flag saluted.

Peaceful coercion Of course the excitement in America was intense, and when Jefferson issued a proclamation closing American ports to British war vessels, it was regarded as preliminary to a formal declaration of war. If it had been, the President would have found himself supported by a united country. But Jefferson was by nature peaceful, and it seems as if his experience in pre-Revolutionary times, with his remembrance of the pressure upon the British through non-importation agreements, must have affected his action now. So reluctant was he to come to the last resort of arms that he first made trial of peaceful coercion, and once embarked upon that method it was difficult to give it up.

The Embargo Upon the President's recommendation and probably in a form drafted by him, Congress adopted an act, in December, 1807, establishing an embargo, which forbade the departure of all vessels in

United States ports for any foreign destination. It could not be regarded as an act for the protection of American shipping, as the shippers did not wish to be protected; the greater the risk, the greater the profit. Evasions of the embargo were frequent, while the successive acts passed for its enforcement became stricter and stricter and involved a usurpation of power by the executive department which was contrary to all Jeffersonian and Democratic theories of government. The British encouraged its evasion, but Napoleon approved the embargo as helping out his Continental system. He even went so far as to assist in enforcing it. By a decree early in 1808 he ordered all American ships in French ports to be seized because they were abroad in contravention of American laws and therefore in all probability engaged in enemy business. Eventually, the failure of the embargo was too patent to be ignored, and one of the last acts of his administration, perhaps the most humiliating of Jefferson's whole career, was signing the law for the repeal of the embargo.

President Madison

At the time of his reëlection to the presidency, Jefferson had let it be known that he would not accept a third term. The question of his successor was interesting but not exciting, for in the state of political parties the candidate supported by the Democratic-Republicans was sure to be successful, and Jefferson's preference was the deciding factor in selecting the man. He was in favor of his Secretary of State, James Madison, who was accordingly elected in 1808 and inaugurated as President the following March. Madison, the master builder of the Constitution, an efficient party leader in Congress, and an able Secretary of State, was still essentially the scholar in politics. A student and thinker, he was lacking in the qualities which make for success in a crisis demanding action. Henry Adams, in his scholarly *History of the United States*, characterized the man and his administration in a brilliant manner by the title to a single chapter, "Madison as Minerva" — the goddess of wisdom and of war is a fitting description of Madison as President.

The act which repealed the embargo had substituted non-intercourse with the British and French, but with a proviso that, if either country should revoke its orders or decrees, trade with that country might be resumed. A new British minister to the United States, David M. Erskine, in his enthusiasm for the restoration of friendly relations, carried out what he conceived to be the spirit rather than the exact wording of his instructions. Madison, in turn, was so eager for peace, that he did not inquire even formally into Erskine's authorization to take such important action, and upon a mere assurance that the orders in council would be revoked he issued a proclamation announcing the resumption of trade with Great Britain. The British Government, however, promptly disavowed the arrangement of Erskine, and Madison had to issue a second proclamation revoking his former one.

The experiment of non-intercourse having been a dismal failure, the opposite policy was tried. Trade with both Great Britain and France was resumed; but the offer was made that if either nation would recall its objectionable orders or decrees, non-intercourse would be reëstablished with the other. This time, in his haste to retrieve his former blunder, Madison allowed himself to be overreached by Napoleon, who promised to revoke the French decrees by a certain date. Relying on this promise only, Madison issued the necessary warning to Great Britain. No evidence was forthcoming that Napoleon ever revoked his decrees, in fact the only news which came was that they were being enforced; but having placed the United States in a false position the President obstinately maintained his stand.

One may differ as to the interpretation of separate incidents or details, but it is difficult not to agree with the late Admiral Mahan's conclusion: —

The United States at this time had abundant justification for war with both France and Great Britain, and it was within the righteous decision of her own policy whether she should declare against either or both; but it is a serious impeachment of a Government's capacity and manfulness when . . . war comes . . . from a series of huckstering attempts to buy off one antagonist or the other, with the result of being fairly over-reached. . . . The course of Great Britain was high-handed, unjust, and not always straightforward; but it was candor itself alongside of Napoleon's.[1]

The approach of war Matters could not continue long in this way, for the humiliating inaction of the Government was steadily spreading discontent throughout the United States. The rising generation, American in spirit, was demanding defense of the national honor. The young, enthusiastic John C. Calhoun was representative of this spirit in the South, and Henry Clay was typical of the West. In the latter section there was a peculiar grievance because of the Indians. The everlasting cause of disturbance was as usual the encroachment of whites upon Indian lands. But that was not the way in which the Westerners looked at it; their point of view is much better shown by Theodore Roosevelt in his sympathetic interpretation of that section, *The Winning of the West*. After recognizing the wrongs which the whites had commit-

[1] *Sea Power in its Relation to the War of 1812*, pp. 249, 250.

ted, he still concludes, "The most ultimately righteous of all wars is a war with savages." So it was regarded by "the men of the Western Waters," and they firmly believed that they would have had no trouble with the Indians if the latter had not been supported and encouraged by Canadians. There may well have been sympathy and support from individuals, but there is not the slightest justification for such a charge against the Canadian authorities. The Westerners, however, did not stop to make any such distinction and demanded war against the British in general, but against the Indians and Canadians in particular.

When the new Congress met in November of 1811 its changed character was shown in the election of Clay as Speaker of the House, and in the adoption of measures that were woefully inadequate, but were unmistakably indicative of a war spirit. It was the presidential year, and it is often asserted that the price of Madison's renomination was his consent to war — in which there is this much of truth, that he thereby obtained the support of the group of "War Hawks." On April 1, 1812, the President recommended and Congress established a general embargo for ninety days as a preliminary to war. On June 1, a war message was sent to Congress and, on June 18, the act declaring war was finally adopted and was signed by the President. The reason for action was simple enough: the limit of endurance had been reached. That war was declared against Great Britain and not against France was due to a combination of circumstances in which the pro-French attitude of the Administration, the personality of the President and the blundering slowness of the British were important elements.

The War of 1812   The War of 1812 was a misfortune for the United States because the time had passed when the people could have been united in supporting it. As John Randolph said in Congress, "We have been embargoed and non-intercoursed almost into a consumption, and this is not the time for battle." It was a misfortune for the British because they were leading the efforts to overthrow Napoleon and they regarded themselves, with some justification, as having been stabbed in the back by a people who should have been helping them. But the greatest misfortune of all was that the war might have been avoided. If there had been cable communication between the two countries it probably would not have come, for two days before the declaration of war by the United States it was announced in the House of Commons that the Orders in Council would be suspended. The British had been ready to yield for some time and were on the point of announcing it, and while the assassination of the Prime Minister, Spencer Perceval, as he was entering the House of Commons on May 11, was an accident of history, it delayed action by the British Government. Even then, if the United States had been adequately represented in London, matters might have been satisfactorily adjusted.

War was undertaken for the purpose of forcing Great Britain to recognize the rights of the United States as a neutral. Henry Clay had boasted that "the militia of Kentucky are alone competent to place Montreal and Upper Canada at your feet," and the Americans entered the war believing that they could conquer Canada and then dictate peace. In fact, it has been charged that the acquisition of Canada was the real purpose of the war, but the several attempts to invade Canada proved dismal failures.

On the other hand, the land efforts of the British were not serious until the battle of Leipsic and the abdication of Napoleon left them free to carry on the war in America with more vigor. Then an expedition from Canada was thwarted by an American victory over the Canadian fleet on Lake Champlain. At the same time a diversion on the Atlantic Coast, meeting with only a show of resistance, found an apparently unexpected opportunity, for the troops marched on Washington, burned the White House and some other public buildings, and then retired. Nothing of real value was accomplished and the only justification for these acts was reprisal for previous American misdoings in Canada. Much was expected from the third expedition against New Orleans, but it was stopped by General Andrew Jackson, who proved himself to be a natural and resourceful leader of men. In the preceding summer he had rallied the men of the Southwest about him and defeated the Creek Indians in the battle of Horseshoe Bend. For the Americans this was one of the most important land events of the war, as it resulted in the opening up of a large amount of Indian territory greatly wanted for settlement. It also made Jackson the hero of the Southwest and helped him in raising troops a second time, and his victory over "Wellington's veterans" at New Orleans in January, 1815, added greatly to his laurels.

Considering the futility of the efforts on both sides, it is easy to sympathize with the Englishman who recorded in his notebook when traveling in America years after the war was over: —

After having been on the field of some of these battles, and read the narratives of them, and having contrasted the small numbers of men engaged in them with the enormous extent of territory and resources of the United States and of Britain, they reminded me of nothing but two furious women scratching each other's cheeks and tearing each other's hair. They bore no reasonable relation to the only conceivable object of war, that of compelling either nation to yield.

The navy On the sea, where they were supposed to be despicably weak, the Americans, to every one's surprise, were wonderfully successful. That is to say, in the naval duels which were the custom of the time, the Americans were generally victorious. This was due to the excellent sailing qualities of their ships, and to the character and ability of their sailors and commanders, but primarily to the fact that of ships of the same class and nominally equal, the American vessels were in almost every case superior in guns and in tonnage. This should not diminish the credit of inflicting defeats upon the hitherto invincible British navy, and it certainly did not lessen the glory of the achievement at the time. It not only atoned for the ignominious failure of the invasions of Canada, but for Americans it left a glamour over the War of 1812 which persists even to this day. The naval victories were astounding and greatly to the credit of the United States, but the superior weight and strength of the British navy produced its inexorable result. The ships of the little American navy were one by one captured or driven to seek permanent refuge in harbors, so that in a little over a year the American flag on all national vessels practically disappeared from the ocean. American privateers were carrying on their legalized piracy with great profit to some of their owners; they were able to inflict considerable damage upon British commerce, and so to raise the rates of insurance, but they did not strike any real blow at the enemy. The British, on the other hand, with their superior navy, were able to establish a blockade of the American coast which was just as effective as they cared to make it. Legitimate American commerce was cut off entirely except where, for reasons of policy, the British were disposed to be lenient.

Hartford Convention It has often been said, and truly, that one of the most remarkable things about the War of 1812 was the opposition to it in the United States. In 1807 the Americans would have been united in a war against England, but in 1812 they were divided in sentiment, and the Madison Administration could not or did not handle the situation effectively. Differences grew into dissension, and sectional opposition grew into or approached treason. In Federalist New England trading with the enemy was a regular practice, so well recognized that the British, in establishing their blockade, exempted New England from it, and Madison referred to this

fact in his messages to Congress. The exaspera-
tion of the New Englanders had been growing
ever since the embargo in 1807. They had opposed the declaration of war as unjustifiable
and as an act of the rankest folly. They
thwarted the Administration in the prosecution
of the war in various ways, and late in 1814
delegates from several of the New England
states planned what was popularly supposed
to be a separation of their section from the
Union. Whatever may have been said or
thought in or outside of the Hartford Convention, the records show only a denunciation
of the Administration, a declaration of principles like that of the Kentucky and Virginia
Resolutions of 1798, and a proposal to amend
the Federal Constitution — characteristic acts
of a disgruntled party or of a section out of
power. The commissioners formally appointed
to carry the protest to Washington reached
there only to be greeted with the news that the
war was over.

The Treaty of Ghent
If the War of 1812 was a misfortune
in its inception, it was equally unfortunate in its ending. Peace was
a blessing, but it saw none of the
things accomplished for which the war had
been fought. In 1814 the causes of war disappeared, as the stopping of the European conflict brought an end to all questions of neutral

trade, and the British were no longer under the necessity of resorting to impressment for the maintenance of their navy. Negotiations for peace were begun immediately after war had been declared, and so when the causes for war were removed there was no reason why peace should not be made. Accordingly the com-missioners arrived at Ghent in August, 1814, and they were able to sign a treaty of peace before the end of the year. In fact, the battle of New Orleans was fought after the treaty had been signed.

Although it settled none of the questions on account of which the war had been fought, the Treaty of Ghent is an all-important docu-ment because it marked the beginning of over a hundred years of peace between the two great English-speaking nations. Growing out of it came the determination of the boundary line between Canada and the United States, to-gether with an agreement that it should not be fortified, and that there should even be disarm-ament on the Great Lakes. Thereby an exam-ple was set for the world of the possibilities of such a policy, which has only been strengthened by its undeniable success.

BIBLIOGRAPHY

Of the general histories Edward Channing's fourth volume (1917) contains the best account of this period and super-sedes his *The Jeffersonian System* (1906). But this does not

dispense with the brilliant piece of historical writing already
referred to in the text, Henry Adams, *History of the United
States, 1801–1817* (9 vols., 1889–1891), which will long remain
the standard authority, especially so far as diplomatic events
are concerned. Of equal importance are the studies of Rear-
Admiral, then Captain, Alfred T. Mahan, *The Influence of
Sea Power upon the French Revolution and Empire, 1793–1812*
(2 vols., 1894), and *Sea Power in its Relations to the War of
1812* (2 vols., 1905). K. C. Babcock, *The Rise of American Nationality* (1906), contains a well-balanced but rather
conventional treatment of the period.

Jefferson is so important a figure of these years that his life
and writings are essential. Channing has an excellent bibliographical note on this subject at the end of chapter IX, and
his statement may well be accepted that James Schouler's
biography of *Thomas Jefferson* (1893) "perhaps best ex-
presses the man."

CHAPTER VI

THE NEW AMERICA

THE War of 1812 may well be taken as the turning-point in the history of the United States; not that the war itself was so important, but the attending circumstances mark the beginning of a new era.

The people First of all an important change had taken place in the people themselves. Immigration had practically ceased forty years before, at the beginning of the fighting between Great Britain and her colonies; it may have revived temporarily with peace, but if so it must have been checked by the European wars. No accurate records were kept, but the estimates in later Census Reports show numbers so small as to be negligible, the increase in population from immigration being not more than one tenth or even one twentieth of one per cent a year. Furthermore, the importation of slaves had been largely stopped by the voluntary action of the individual states, and then entirely prohibited by the Federal Government in 1807.

These conditions gave the necessary opportunity for the forces of assimilation to work, among which a steady natural increase of the population, undisturbed by foreign immigration, and the busy, prosperous, and contented state of the people were important. Accordingly, in the course of forty years the foreign elements in the United States seem to have been so largely absorbed that for the first time there arose an American people with something like a national spirit, and displaying many traits that have come to be known as American; there seemed almost to be a distinct physical type discernible. The War of 1812 had revealed a people sadly divided as to the wisdom or justice of the war, but it was a difference of sections and of sectional interests rather than of racial or national strains. Even with public opinion divided, this war was no exception to the rule that war stimulates patriotism, and in this the early naval successes and Jackson's victory at New Orleans had done their part by arousing enthusiasm and pride.

One of the strong nationalizing forces was the westward movement of population with its mingling and mixing of classes and races on the frontier, but that migration was of equal importance in other ways by its very extent and size. The flood of settlers that broke across the mountains at the close of the Revolution had never slackened; in fact, it steadily increased in volume. By 1810 there were 1,500,-000 people on the Western waters; and in 1820, out of a total population in the United States of 9,500,000, nearly one third, or over 3,000,000, were in the West. Population west of the Alleghenies not merely relatively but actually increased more rapidly than the population of the rest of the United States. The condition thereby created is all-important in understanding the New America, and especially its industrial and commercial situation.

Industry The Embargo of 1807 and the Jeffersonian policy of peaceful coercion through commercial restrictions were responsible for a great increase in manufacturing in the United States. There had always been a large amount of household manufactures in America, even in colonial times; but since the introduction of cotton machinery in 1789 by Samuel Slater, and especially when the spread of these factories was hastened by the invention of the cotton gin in 1793, there had been a gradual transfer of industry from the household or small shop to the factory. Then came a sudden stimulus from the embargo, which was strengthened by the fact that it was supported as a national measure, so that instead of importing foreign goods it became a mark of patriotism to use those of domestic manufacture.

One of the popular ways of supporting the embargo was by wearing home-made clothing. In spite of all the efforts of such men as Washington and Colonel David Humphreys, and even of agricultural societies, there was little fine wool produced in the country, so that Americans were dependent upon outside sources both for their supply of raw wool and for woolen manufactures. An emergency had now arisen where supplying home demands was a patriotic necessity. In 1808 a British secret agent in the United States reported to the Lieutenant-Governor of Halifax: —

The President had a great Levy on the 4th of July, and as another Tub to the Whale, he had on a Homespun Coat. To hear the Talk about this Coat at Washington and Georgetown would lead to the supposition, that these silly people supposed there was a sort of magic in it, which would work the ruin of the Manufacturers of Great Britain.

President Madison at his inauguration set a similar example; he was spoken of as "'a walking argument for the encouragement of the manufacture of native wool.' His coat had been made on the farm of Colonel Humphreys, and his waistcoat and small clothes on that of Chancellor Livingston, all from the wool of merino sheep raised in the country."

The ultimate result of all this was an insistent demand for a greater supply of finer grades of wool, and a consequent improvement in the breed of sheep, until wool-growing and wool-manufacturing became an important industry in the United States. And this is only one illustration of what was taking place in other directions as well, for the rapid development of manufactures was made possible by the increased capital that had accrued from the neutral trade. When a restrictive commercial policy was adopted, new outlets for the use of capital had to be found and, as a patriotic service was thereby rendered, factories became a favored form of investment. The moment the war was over, however, European manufactured goods poured into the United States to such an extent that these infant industries were threatened with extinction, and the men who had forced the declaration of war now recognized their responsibility in the changed state of affairs. Accordingly, among the earliest measures passed after the war was a new tariff act which is commonly regarded as the first protective tariff in the United States, because protection, having been a minor element in the previous acts, now became a major purpose and of increasing importance in comparison with revenue. It may be regarded as the last step toward establishing manufactures in the United States, and therewith the country was passing out of the age of homespun and into the age of machinery.

Cotton-growing Significant as this development may have been, it probably was not the most important phase of the transformation taking place in the United States. Where so many and such great changes were occurring it is difficult to choose any one in preference to another, but it seems as if the fundamental factor in precipitating other changes at this time was the increase in cotton-growing and its spread into the Southwest. The invention of the cotton gin in 1793 had made profitable the growing of upland or short staple cotton; so immediate were its effects that before 1800 cotton had surpassed tobacco, as the leading crop of the South, and by 1816 it was nearly double the latter in value. For the growing of this staple more land was needed, and the fertile lands of western Georgia, Alabama, and Mississippi were greatly wanted. Therein lies the explanation of most of the Indian troubles in the South, and of the tremendous popularity of Jackson's victory over the Creeks, already referred to, which resulted in the cession of a large amount of Indian lands. As fast as any such territory was opened up it was rapidly taken by the whites for cotton production.

Slavery The subject of cotton-growing inevitably leads to the consideration of slavery, for the two were closely connected. Even at the present day labor is the most important element in the cost of cotton production, and whether or not cotton can be grown successfully with white labor is irrelevant, for in the early eighteenth century it was not believed possible, at least in the South. Negro labor was regarded as essential, and slavery was the legal system adjusting the relations of the negroes and their employers. In the next place, negro labor attained its greatest efficiency when organized and handled in gangs, and so the tendency was to concentrate on plantations and to specialize in the production of crops. It was the spread of the plantation system — some would say the spread of cotton-growing, but the two were almost synonymous — that changed the attitude of the South on the subject of slavery. Thirty years before this, leading men of that section, such as Washington and Jefferson, had regarded slavery as only a temporary evil. But the increase of cotton-growing, with its apparent necessity of negro labor, seemed to fasten slavery on the South; at any rate, the spread of cotton culture into the Southwest was accompanied by a corresponding spread of slavery. Furthermore, it was a different slavery from that of the old patriarchal system in Virginia, for it was commercialized. It was also the spread of cotton-growing and of the plantation system to the upland region that united the different sections of the South in a common economic interest, out of which came later the "Solid South." And finally it was the expansion of slavery that aroused the North and first brought the slavery question to the fore.

It is easy to write diatribes against the institution of slavery; but in the early nineteenth century it was considered to be a part of the established order. Cruelty to slaves was regarded very much as cruelty to animals is at the present time and seems to have been one of the main reasons for opposition to the slave trade. But the right of holding negroes in servitude was not generally regarded as debatable; for most people, it was not a moral question. Slavery had been practically universal in the colonies, but it did not work well in the North and so it was gradually abolished in New England and as far south as Pennsylvania, until the boundary of that state, which had been surveyed by Mason and Dixon and was known by their names, became the accidental dividing line between slave and free in the East. As for the West, the Ordinance of 1787 had prohibited slavery northwest of the Ohio River, but when the Ordinance was extended over territories in the South that provision was omitted. Accordingly the Ohio River became the continuation of the Mason and Dixon line beyond the Allegheny Mountains.

The Missouri Compromise

When the slavery question arose in the United States it was not at all over the abolition of slavery, but over the extension of slavery into the new territories which were opening up in the West, especially in the Louisiana Purchase. It sprang out of the antagonism of interests between two sections of the country caused by the fact that in one section negro labor in the form of slavery lay at the foundation of the whole industrial and social structure and in the other it did not. The State of Louisiana itself was so far to the south that it was admitted into the Union in 1812 without any difficulty arising on the subject of slavery; but when Missouri was ready for admission the case was different. The new state was opposite the mouth of the Ohio River and so on a debatable line, while conditions were different in 1819 from what they had been a few years before. The matter was finally settled by the well-known Missouri Compromise in 1820, according to which Missouri itself was allowed to come into the Union with slavery, but all other states north of the continuation of her southern boundary line should be free.

The opposition of the North to the extension of slavery was an important fact, but equally significant was the changed attitude toward the institution on the part of the South. In 1785 Jefferson had hoped and believed that slavery would come to an end in his section. At the time of the Missouri Compromise, 1820, while he would have been glad to see general emancipation, he qualified his statement: "But as it is, we have the wolf by the ears, and we can neither hold him, nor safely let him go. Justice is in one scale, and self-preservation in the other."

Internal commerce As already noticed, the tendency of Southerners was to devote their plantations to producing a few staple crops which necessitated their obtaining food and other needed supplies from outside sources. The Northwest was a great region from which the South drew farming products, and whereas the Southerners had formerly raised large quantities of live-stock, now they imported their horses, mules, cattle, and hogs from Kentucky and Tennessee, as well as from states farther north and west. Both the Northwest and the South looked to New England and the Middle States for manufactured goods, and those sections in turn called upon the Northwest for foodstuffs and upon the South for such of its products as they could use. In this interchange of commodities it was of great advantage that the South could dispose of its surplus cotton at a profit, because of the great demand from England and from Europe after 1815.

The substance of the whole matter is that the United States was developing, for the first time to any considerable extent, domestic commerce involving specialization of sections. Speaking broadly, different sections were devoting themselves to certain classes of products or of industries, and were exchanging their wares. It meant a division of labor between the planters of the South, the farmers of the North, and the manufacturers of the East; and it meant the development of an important trade between those sections, greater in amount and more lucrative than the old colonial commerce or even than the neutral trade had been.

In a recent article, Professor Turner has written that "The frontier and the section are two of the most fundamental factors in American history"; and again, that "Sections are more important than states in shaping the underlying forces of American history." It may well be that an appreciation of the strength of sectionalism is essential to a correct understanding of the development of the United States, but a greater force than sectionalism was here at work. Internal commerce was an all-important factor in developing nationality. This is what the economists have in mind when they say that the United States was at this time passing out of its colonial condition, that is, out of a condition of industrial dependence. The Americans still had to look abroad for markets for some of their surplus products and for the purchase of some manufactured articles; but they were increasingly conscious of the fact that, for the first time in their history, they were becoming industrially and commercially more and more sufficient unto themselves. They were able to supply an increasing proportion of the raw materials they needed and of the manufactured goods as well. It was not merely national enthusiasm aroused by the war; there was a new consciousness of genuine national completeness.

The steamboat In the year of the embargo, another event of equal importance occurred, — and few saw any connection, — Robert Fulton demonstrated the possibility of successfully using steam in water transportation for commercial purposes, by running the Clermont from New York to Albany. Not long afterwards, in 1811, the building of a steamboat on the Ohio River opened a new chapter in the history of the West; the era of upstream navigation had begun. Without such assistance it does not seem possible that internal commerce could have developed in the United States; and certainly not in the way in which it did. When two to three million people were living west of the Allegheny Mountains, and offered the markets which Eastern manufacturers were seeking, the demand for improved means of transportation between the sections was inevitable and soon became irresistible. It was only too evident that the Old National Road, opened shortly after the War of 1812 and largely used, could not supply the needs of the time; something more and something better must be had. The building of a waterway from East to West, which had earlier seemed a dream of visionaries, now became an apparent necessity.

Erie Canal New York unquestionably possessed, in the Mohawk Valley, the easiest route for a canal to the West. The ground had been surveyed, plans had been drawn, and the people of the state, mainly through the efforts and enthusiasm of De Witt Clinton, had been brought to the point where they were ready to undertake the work. But the United States Government was also concerned, for this was a matter of national importance. It was proposed that the bonus received from the United States Bank, together with the profits derived from the Government stock, should be devoted to the improvement of transportation and it was understood that the New York canal would be a favored project. A bill to that effect passed both houses of Congress but, though in sympathy with its purpose, President Madison felt obliged, as one of the very last acts of his administration, to veto it on constitutional grounds. The views of his successor, James Monroe, who had been Secretary of State, were known to be similar, and so if anything was to be done, it must be by the state or as a private enterprise. Accordingly the Erie Canal was begun by the State of New York in 1817; it was completed in 1825; and the whole course of American development was affected. Transportation between Albany and Buffalo was reduced to one tenth of its former cost, and while the cut in rates could not always be as large, freight charges to the West everywhere were greatly reduced. This lowered the price of manufactured goods in practically all the Western country, especially in the region reached by the Great Lakes, and thereby not only greatly extended the market for Eastern manufactures, but ultimately brought about the transportation of foodstuffs from the West to the East. New York City was finally established as the emporium of the United States, and not only was the value of property along the canal greatly increased but, most surprising of all, the canal itself proved to be a financial success. The bare enumeration of these facts is sufficient to account for the similar undertakings in Pennsylvania, Maryland, and even in the South, and for the stimulus to canal-building all over the country, especially in the Northwest.

With all of these projects before them discussions were sure to arise over the interpretation of the Constitution as to governmental authority. It was not merely a question of internal improvements at national expense; the undertakings were going beyond the confines of a single state and the powers of the National Government were being invoked. It was in these years that the Supreme Court, under the domination of its Chief Justice, John Marshall, handed down some of its most important decisions, looking toward the extension of the powers of the central Government; and among these decisions none were more important than those involving interstate commerce, in which the broad principles were laid down upon which practically all interstate commerce decisions have since been rendered. It is no wonder that there should come a demand just at this time for printing the journal of the convention which framed the Constitution of the United States, in order that as much as possible should be known of what was and what was not within the power of the Federal Government.

Enough has been given to show why the War of 1812 is justly referred to as the "second war of independence," for it marks the real beginning of freedom from industrial and commercial dependence upon Great Britain and Europe. It is of even greater consequence that for the first time in the history of the United States the people of the Atlantic Coast appreciated the importance to them of the West and that they were willing to recognize it. Therein lies the significance of the saying that the people of the East, turning their backs on Europe, faced squarely around and looked toward the West.

Foreign relations   The independent and new national spirit of Americans was manifesting itself in other directions and nowhere more markedly than by an increased vigor and strength in foreign affairs. When a commercial dispute arose in 1816 with two Canadian provinces, and an effort was made to force the carrying of certain products to American ports in British vessels only, the United States, instead of submitting, promptly prohibited the importation of these products altogether, and the Canadians yielded. It was a matter of minor importance, but it was regarded as a triumph over Great Britain, because it was believed to be a declaration that Americans were strong enough to carry out a policy of retaliation against a great commercial power. And so John Quincy Adams could write in his diary that while it was "upon a very insignificant subject . . . it was one of the most significant acts" of the United States "since the Declaration of Independence."

Monroe Doctrine It was an assertion of this same nationalism that underlay and gave strength to the Monroe Doctrine. During the Napoleonic Wars, especially after the establishment of Joseph Bonaparte upon the throne of Spain, the long-existing discontent in the Spanish colonies of Central and South America had culminated in revolution, and in the course of a few years all except Cuba and Porto Rico had established their independence. Great Britain took advantage of the situation to develop trade relations with the newly independent states, and while not recognizing the independence of the Spanish-American republics, she had declared neutrality. The interests of the United States were similar to those of the British, but American sympathy was more fully aroused. There was a general belief among Americans, stimulated by the propaganda of Francisco de Miranda, a "flaming Son of Liberty," that the independence of Spanish America was merely a continuation and development of the independence which the United States had established, and it therefore appealed to American ideals and to American pride.

Action would have come much earlier if it had not been that negotiations were under way for the transfer of the Floridas from Spain. Ultimate ownership in the United States was inevitable, which Spain was brought to realize, and a treaty for that purpose was signed in 1819. Owing to various complications, ratification of the treaty was delayed in both Spain and the United States, so that it was not finally completed until March, 1822, and then President Monroe immediately recommended to Congress the recognition of the South American republics.

When the restoration of conditions in Europe was under way, France had been entrusted with the reëstablishment of the monarchy in Spain, and had successfully carried out her measures. It was also planned to restore the Spanish colonies to their former dependence, but this was not regarded with approval either in England or in the United States. Another factor entering into the situation was a result of Russian aggressiveness on the western coast of North America, which manifested itself in an effort to enlarge the boundaries of Alaska, whereby a protectorate would have been established over a large area on the Pacific Coast. As this could not be accepted quietly by Great Britain and the United States, the two countries here also were working in harmony.

It was no new idea which was put forward,

as it had been developing for a long time; nor was it the work of any one man. It may have lain in Washington's mind, Jefferson expressed it plainly, while Henry Clay and John Quincy Adams can be immediately connected with its formulation. Whatever its authorship and origin may have been, it was in a message to Congress in 1823 that the President of the United States gave expression to what has ever since been known as the Monroe Doctrine. In explaining foreign relations President Monroe described the Russian situation on the Pacific Coast, declaring that the matter was being handled successfully in the ordinary diplomatic way; he stated that a similar result had been achieved in negotiations between Russia and Great Britain; and then added that the occasion seemed proper for "asserting, as a principle in which the rights and interests of the United States are involved, that the American continents, by the free and independent condition which they have assumed and maintain, are henceforth not to be considered as subjects for future colonization by any European powers."

After taking up several other matters in his message, the President came to South American affairs, and stated: —

In the wars of the European powers, in matters relating to themselves, we have never taken any

part, nor does it comport with our policy so to do.
. . . The political system of the allied powers is
essentially different from that of America. This
difference proceeds from that which exists in their
respective governments. And to the defence of our
own, . . . this whole nation is devoted. We owe it,
therefore, to candor, and to the amicable relations
existing between the United States and those powers, to declare, that we should consider any attempt
on their part to extend their system to any portion
of this hemisphere, as dangerous to our peace and
safety. With the existing colonies or dependencies
of any European power, we have not interfered, and
shall not interfere. But with the governments who
have declared their independence, and maintained
it, and whose independence we have, on great consideration, and on just principles, acknowledged,
we could not view any interposition for the purpose
of oppressing them, or controlling, in any other
manner, their destiny, by any European power,
in any other light than as the manifestation of an
unfriendly disposition towards the United States.
. . . It is impossible that the allied powers should
extend their political system to any portion of either
continent, without endangering our peace and happiness.

The Monroe Doctrine marks the coming of
age of the United States, when that country,
for the first time, was able to command the
respect of Europe. It makes no difference that
the declaration might not have been effective
had it not been known that it was supported by
Great Britain and backed by the British fleet.
Whatever the extraneous circumstances may
have been, the United States said to Europe

"Hands off!" and the European powers observed the injunction. To the people of the United States, aside from the pride they took in the position their country had assumed, the appeal of the Monroe Doctrine was a double one: It realized their ideal of themselves as leaders in the cause of liberty, and the practical value of "America for the Americans" was perfectly evident. Even the indefinite character of the doctrine has proved to be one of its greatest assets, as it has been possible in a crisis to employ it in unexpected ways. It is an interesting process of development, that the difference in political systems, upon which action was justified in 1823, is hardly valid now; whereas an almost incidental declaration in connection with Russia, that no future colonization could be permitted, has become the important feature.

BIBLIOGRAPHY

There is not much to be added to the bibliographical notes of previous chapters. Although the books on the subjects of slavery and the Monroe Doctrine are innumerable, some are of little value and many are not of general interest. F. J. Turner, *The Rise of the New West, 1819–1829* (1906), is the best single volume covering the period, and contains an excellent account of the formulation of the Monroe Doctrine. A. C. Coolidge, *The United States as a World Power* (1908), has a very good chapter on the significance of the Monroe Doctrine in the light of its subsequent developments. E. L. Bogart, *Economic History of the United States* (2d edition 1912), becomes increasingly useful from this time on.

Among the special histories might be noted C. W. Wright, *Wool Growing and the Tariff* (1910), and F. W. Taussig's authoritative *Tariff History of the United States* (of which the 6th edition appeared in 1913).

CHAPTER VII

DEMOCRACY

It is evident that a profound change had taken place in the United States of which only certain external forms have been mentioned here. When accompanied as it was by an equally great change in the inner life of the people, it seems as if almost a transformation of Americans was in process and to follow it is absorbingly interesting. Perhaps the most striking feature was the way in which the practical cast of American progress was stamping itself unmistakably upon the things of the spirit. Henry Adams, in commenting upon some of the different aspects of American character after the War of 1812, wrote with keen appreciation at the close of his *History*: "Paradoxical as it may seem, it was the pursuit of gain that made men more generous, tolerant, and liberal in their dealings and their relations with their fellow men, and not the teachings of the church. As commerce increased its hold that of the church relaxed." Conservative church-goers were shocked by the unorthodox and godless behavior of the mass of the people, whereas the liberally inclined insisted that they were displaying a more genuine and therefore a more deeply religious spirit. It was a world-old difference that was manifesting itself, but the turn which it took was indicative of the time as well as of American conditions. If New England was not the leader it was typical of the rest of the country, and there the old religious ideas were taking on more of an ethical cast, they were becoming more practical, and men were turning in the direction of philanthropy and social reform.

Politics   In the political sphere the effect of changed conditions had been to undermine the old privileged class. The late William Graham Sumner has been quoted as saying that Americans were not free and equal merely because Jefferson put it into the Declaration of Independence; but Jefferson could put it into the Declaration of Independence because the economic relations existing in America made the members of society to all intents and purposes free and equal. But it is necessary to go one step farther and to realize that the Americans were not free and equal in 1776, and that it was not until the generation of the Revolution had passed away that opportunities were given for the leveling forces in the United States to produce their full results. Rufus King, who was of the old order, but able to recognize and accept the changed situation, said to the rising generation: —

You young men who have been born since the Revolution, look with horror upon the name of a King, and upon all propositions for a strong government. It was not so with us. We were born the subjects of a King, and were accustomed to subscribe ourselves "His Majesty's most faithful subjects."

A little later George Combe, who has already been quoted to the same effect, finished the story: —

But the condition of affairs is now changed. The generation trained to obedience under monarchical institutions is extinct; a race occupies the field which has been reared under the full influence of democracy.

Josiah Quincy said that it had taken a half-century after the Declaration of Independence "to reach a vital belief that the people and not gentlemen (using the word, of course, in its common and narrow sense) are to govern this country."

Democracy The old régime had been strongly enough entrenched to withstand the attacks upon its position for a considerable time, but the progress of democracy was steady and inexorable. Test oaths, religious requirements, and property qualifications for both office-holding and voting were disappearing one after another; representation was being apportioned on the basis of the whole population rather than on the number of electors or taxpayers; and the offices were increasing that were to be filled by popular election instead of by appointment of governor or legislature. The West was in a large measure responsible for the way things were turning. By 1820 there were nine states beyond the Allegheny Mountains out of a total of twenty-four, and with the equality of conditions existing there, when those states formed their constitutions they had taken the lead in extending these democratic provisions. This in turn reacted upon the older states in the East, both by way of example and by actual pressure through loss of population, as many citizens were leaving because conditions were preferable in the West, and one of the attractions was political equality. State after state in the East, even the most conservative, revised its constitution.

Connecticut　　Typical of the old order and of the new conditions as well was Connecticut. At the time of the Revolution that state, having enjoyed the greatest degree of self-government under her colonial charter, was not obliged to frame a new constitution; she simply continued the charter government. The people of the colony and of the state were supposed to have control because they elected their own governor and both houses of the legislature; but by the second decade of the nineteenth century, Connecticut's government was regarded as essentially aristocratic under the control of a privileged class. The liberal government of 1776 had become antiquated by 1816. Ever since the success of the Democratic-Republicans in the election of Jefferson to the presidency discontent in Connecticut had been growing. The prospect was so discouraging, however, that Pierrepont Edwards, "a leader of the Democrats" in Congress, is said to have exclaimed, "As well attempt to revolutionize the kingdom of heaven as the State of Connecticut!" Yet by 1818 the liberal elements were strong enough to force the framing of a new constitution which was submitted to the people and adopted. While the spread of democratic principles was largely due to changing economic conditions, the immediate reform in the government of Connecticut — and the same would be true of other New England states — was brought about through a combination of dissenting Baptists and Methodists, with the support of the Episcopalians, all of whom had a common grievance against the Federalist Congregationalist hierarchy.

Indicative also of the new order of things was the submission of Connecticut's constitution to popular vote for approval. Massachusetts and New Hampshire had adopted this

method at the time of the Revolution, but
Connecticut was the first to revive the practice.
Maine, New York, Rhode Island, and even
Virginia followed suit, and the submission of
constitutions for popular approval became the
established order of procedure.

Undoubtedly the process of democratization
was helped along by the panic of 1819. A financial crisis was a very natural occurrence in the
process of adjustment to radically new industrial conditions, but it was sharp while it lasted
and distress was widespread. Accordingly, as
always happens, increased discontent was of
material assistance in bringing about political
changes.

But whatever explanations are offered, they
cannot detract from the importance of the
commonly accepted statement that in the
course of a relatively few years after the War
of 1812 democracy became an established fact
in the United States. There is also no doubt
that most Americans took great pride in it. To
the eyes of many foreign travelers, however,
it was not producing attractive results, nor
did it seem to maintain an efficient government. They might well have quoted Fisher
Ames: —

A monarchy is like a merchantman. You get on
board and ride the wind and tide in safety and
elation but, by and by, you strike a reef and go

down. But democracy is like a raft. You never sink, but, damn it, your feet are always in the water![1]

Yet those same travelers admitted the general happiness and contentment of the people, and they commented favorably upon the extension of education which followed the widening of the suffrage.

Political parties   The Federalists had been the upholders of the old order, and after the War of 1812 their party dwindled away; it was commonly said that they died out because of the success of their principles in the hands of their opponents. When the Democratic-Republicans found themselves obliged by the force of circumstances to adopt a broad construction of the Constitution, and when the Democratic-Republican administration proved successful, there was no longer an excuse for a party with Federalist principles. James Monroe had been a rival of Madison for the presidency in 1808, and was regarded as his inevitable successor on the latter's retirement. Accordingly there was little opposition to his election in 1816, and whatever opposition there was had entirely disappeared in 1820, so that all the electoral votes with a single exception were cast for his reëlection, and that

[1] Cited by G. M. Wrong, "The Creation of the Federal System in Canada," in *The Federation of Canada* (Toronto, 1917), p. 21.

exception was made for purely sentimental reasons, one of the electors declaring that no one
but Washington should have the honor of
unanimous election. It was the absence of
party divisions that was mainly responsible for
calling Monroe's administrations the "Era
of Good Feeling."

But the harmonious course of politics was
not allowed to lapse into monotony, and one
of the interesting incidents of the spread of
democracy in America was the manner in
which the control of affairs formerly exercised
by leading men was taken away. Originally
the influential men of a community had succeeded in having their preferences fulfilled
or their will carried out largely by force of
character and the strength of their social position. With the development of parties these
same men would meet together and the word
would then be spread abroad that the party
would do thus and so, or that party members
would vote for such and such candidates.
As party machinery was built up these groups
tended to become more and more of an organization. It was natural that the leaders of the
party who were in office should take it upon
themselves to determine matters of policy, and
the largest numbers were in the legislature.
The meetings of the legislative party leaders
came to be known as caucuses, and so it hap-

pened that with the awakening of democracy there came a revolt against the domination of the caucus.

Andrew Jackson The revolt was greatly helped by the presidential elections of 1824 and 1828. At the end of Monroe's second term the fact of there being but one party did not mean that every one was in accord. Factions within the party were numerous and so many candidates for the highest office arose that only a few months before the election a dozen or more names were mentioned; it is commonly known, therefore, as the "scrub race for the presidency." As always the contest narrowed down to comparatively few, and when the campaign was really under way only five men could be considered in the race. John C. Calhoun withdrew with the understanding that he should be made Vice-President, but even then no one was able to secure a majority of the electoral votes. In some states the electors had been chosen by popular vote, but in most they were chosen by the legislatures. Where the people had voted, Andrew Jackson was the favorite, having been put forward as the opponent of "the Virginia Dynasty," and he also received a larger number of electoral votes than any other candidate. His supporters felt that on the face of the returns he should be made President, but the

Constitution provided in the contingency of no electoral majority that the choice should be made by the House of Representatives from the "five highest on the list" returned by the electoral college. A subsequent amendment had changed this to the highest three, which in this case eliminated Henry Clay, who was fourth and would probably have been the strongest candidate before the House. The third candidate was William H. Crawford, of Georgia, who had been hindered rather than helped by receiving the formal nomination of the Congressional caucus, and he was now out of the running, if for no other reason, because of a stroke of paralysis. Accordingly, the choice lay between Jackson and John Quincy Adams, and as Clay threw his influence to the support of the latter Adams was elected. In one way, it was unfortunate that Clay accepted the office of Secretary of State, regarded as the position of the heir apparent, for the cry of corrupt bargaining was at once raised; and although no proof could be adduced in support of the charge, it put the Adams Administration on the defensive from the start.

No sooner was the question of the presidency settled in 1825, than the Jackson men began their campaign for the next election, four years later. It was not a question of principles, but of personalities. It was Jackson against the

Administration, against Adams and Clay, both or either of them. Yet out of this conflict of personalities, accidentally as it were, party principles developed. Clay championed a protective tariff and internal improvements as a part of his "American system," and to Adams, a former Federalist, such principles were altogether congenial. Accordingly the Adams and Clay factions joined forces on these questions; in opposition to the Democratic-Republicans they became National Republicans, and a few years later they took the name of Whigs.

At the time the question was largely a personal one, and yet, although "Hurrah for Jackson!" was the rallying cry of the campaign, there was something more than that and more even than the uprising against the old order expressed in Jackson's dictum, "Let the people rule." Senator Martin Van Buren, trained in the New York school of politics which was already becoming famous, had joined the Jackson forces and was one of what would now be called the managers of his campaign. Just how much credit belongs to him it would be difficult to say, but New York methods were followed, and back of the enthusiasm of the campaign was organization, to which much of Jackson's overwhelming success in 1828 must be attributed. It was a victory of the South and West, especially of the latter; it was a victory for democracy; but it was also a victory of organized politics.

Professional politicians
Organization required workers and when they had been successful those workers demanded their reward. Accordingly, with the inauguration of Jackson we see the "spoils system," the giving of Government offices to successful party workers, frankly adopted by the Federal Administration. It was merely an application to the national field on a large scale of what long had been the practice locally or on a small scale, but it seems to mark the rise of a class of professional politicians. These men were not like the old ruling class whose members were in politics largely from a sense of duty and public service, or for the honor of it, or even for the sake of power; but they were in politics as a business, not for the irregular profits to be derived therefrom, but to make a living.

The Marquis de Lafayette has always stood to Americans as the embodiment of the French aid that enabled them to win their independence and, when he made his triumphal return to the United States in 1824, he was interested and amused at the greetings of his fellow veterans of the Revolution. "What do you think," he said, "is the question which these Revolutionary soldiers almost invariably ask me? It is this, 'What do you do for a living?' and sometimes the inquiry comes, 'What was your father's business?'" Upon which Josiah Quincy commented, "Now, everybody is working for a living in America, — that is, pursuing some money-getting trade or profession, — and the people do not understand how it can be otherwise in the older countries." The salient American trait so vividly portrayed in this anecdote not only lies at the very foundation of American life and character, but offers an explanation of the course that politics took in the United States.

It is becoming customary to ascribe the development of the nervous, hurried energy of the American people to the period after the War of 1812. Whether one accepts this or traces its origin farther back in earlier effects of a stimulating climate, all can agree that the Americans at this time were a busy people, absorbed in their work. When the first enthusiasm of overthrowing the caucus had passed, it was only human nature, but it was also characteristic of them, that Americans were unwilling to bother with politics except to vote, and that they were glad to have matters managed for them. And so there were two classes of men: those interested in business and a smaller class interested in politics; or it might be said that all were interested in business only some were making a business of politics. It is a fact to be remembered at every stage of American history from that day to this.

Influence of the West
The influence of the West upon the growth of democracy has been shown and it was responsible, to an equal extent, for the distinguishing character of certain other changes that were taking place. There was a geographic as well as a political and social force. The Federalists as a class had been pro-British in sympathy; indeed, they were allied in many cases by financial interests and family ties, so that English social ideals had dominated in the United States. Under the new conditions Americans were freeing themselves from outside influences, they were progressing in their own way, and the farther west they went the more independent was their development. Emerson could write in 1844: "Europe stretches to the Alleghenies; America lies beyond." Lord Bryce, in *The American Commonwealth*, has said that "The West may be called the most distinctly American part of America, because the points in which it differs from the East are the points in which America as a whole differs from Europe."

No more striking illustration of the peculiarly American character of this development can be found than that pointed out by President Hadley: "Men with a hundred and sixty acres of land were not likely to pass laws which would interfere with the rights of property, and particularly of landed property. . . . The immigrant found it easy to get land; he found it hard to get capital." Expansion of democracy in the United States was accompanied by the protection of property rights and by the encouragement of capital.

American traits In the things of the spirit also this influence was manifest. Liberty, equality, and opportunity were fundamental in American life. They were essential in the establishment of American democracy, and when combined with other elements it seems as if many of the characteristics that have come to be known as American were being revealed in the period under consideration, that is, in the second generation after the Revolution. At the basis lay the qualities of bravery, resourcefulness, and self-reliance, which were indispensable to the maintenance of life upon the frontier, and all America passed through the frontier stage. Adaptability was a product rather than an original quality.

Quite early one finds contemporary comments upon the spirit of gambling in the United States, but gaming was prevalent the world over and does not describe the passion which animated, and still animates, the American people. The very opportunities that were offered in the new country led to recklessness. Failure was not disastrous. It only meant beginning over again, and men grew accustomed to taking chances. Some foreign observers were discerning enough to see that Americans enjoyed the contest; they loved the game; and they also played the game to win. One of the shrewdest characterizations ever made was that an American likes better than anything else to make a dollar where no one else has seen the chance or where somebody else has failed. Franz Löher commented upon the fact that every American had a *business*, whether he were a clergyman, a lawyer, a physician, or a tradesman, at which he worked unceasingly. He was writing in 1847, but he was able then to say that nothing was farther from the truth than that love of money was the object of this tireless effort. Nowhere else did they give so much to schools and churches and charitable institutions. Wealth meant power, but it was chiefly prized as the proof and the emblem of success.

It is easy to see how out of the conditions existing other traits developed such as cheerfulness, good-nature, generosity, and above all a deeply rooted belief in an opportunity for every man, a conviction which ultimately led to the principle of fair play and the doctrine of the square deal.

Still other characteristics sprang from the youthfulness of the people; as a nation they were young, but individually they were young also. The men and women who were colonizing the West and building there the American Nation were young in years; they were filled with hope and with enthusiasm. Even foreign immigration was composed "neither of single men, nor of old people, nor of middle-aged people dragging children along with them, but, for the most part, of young couples seeking a new home, fondly encouraging each other, strong in health and spirits, not driven from birthplace by the fear of want, but attracted to a new place by motives of ambition for themselves and for children to come."[1]

A sense of humor is conspicuous in American temperament, and whether it comes from an appreciation of the incongruous, or from scorn for any lack of adaptability, from a "magnificent spirit of exaggeration," from a surplus of nervous energy seeking relief, or from any other of the numerous explanations, the necessary conditions seemed to exist in the new country. Boisterous and rough in those early years, time has served to soften and refine American humor, and apparently without weakening it to any extent. A similar process of refinement was going on in the manners of

[1] E. G. Wakefield, *View of the Art of Colonization* (1849).

the American people which unquestionably were deficient in early days. Yet de Tocqueville saw that equality of conditions in the United States was certain, in the course of time, to increase civility and to improve manners, because the basis of all good manners was there in the respect for others simply as men and women irrespective of class.

But equality was not an unmixed blessing, even to such a sympathetic critic as de Tocqueville, for he also wrote: "When I survey this countless multitude of beings shaped in each other's likeness, amidst whom nothing rises and nothing falls, the sight of such universal uniformity saddens and chills me." Apparently Carlyle was impressed in the same way when he gave vent to the sarcasm: "They have begotten, with a rapidity beyond recorded example, eighteen millions of the greatest bores ever seen in the world before — that hitherto is their feat in History."

The haste with which things were done led, of course, to superficiality; many critics mention it; and the difference in the point of view is of almost equal significance. Foreigners, and especially Englishmen, asked why bridges were built of wood instead of stone, and the question *amused* as well as interested Americans. It was this same haste, however, that stimulated the American genius for invention through the exercise of his ingenuity in devices for saving time and labor.

The Americans might have been superficial, but they were serious in their purposes.

Especially the Americans have great earnestness of character; . . . I think I have never seen more of it in any people. Their character, like their climate, has great decision about it; it may be hot, it may be cold; but when it is cold it freezes, and when it is hot it burns.[1]

They were idealists, too, and in its own way the West again played an important part. In the words of Professor Turner: —

The Western man believed in the manifest destiny of his country. . . . the frontiersman's dream was prophetic. In spite of his rude, gross nature, this early Western man was an idealist withal. He dreamed dreams and beheld visions. He had faith in man, hope for democracy, belief in America's destiny, unbounded confidence in his ability to make his dreams come true.[2]

If there was a composite type developing it was in the Middle West, and it would have shown inheritances from every section of the country: the ethical religious ideals of New England, the social standards of the South, the practical and commercial aims of the Middle States, and the Western insistence upon equality.

[1] Reed and Matheson, *Narrative of Visit to the American Churches*, II (1835), p. 281.
[2] "The Problem of the West," in *The Atlantic Monthly*, September, 1896.

BIBLIOGRAPHY

Attention has already been called to the standard works covering the events of this chapter. Most of the material upon American characteristics was taken from accounts of travelers, of which there is a valuable list in the *Cambridge History of American Literature* (Part I, 1917), but especial reference should be made to Alexis C. H. de Tocqueville, *De la Démocratie en Amérique* (2 vols., Paris, 1835–1840; translated by Reeve and by Bowen), which still remains the classical interpretation of American democracy of that time. The writer is also conscious of having used later works with profit, notably, A. Maurice Low, *The American People* (2 vols., 1909–1911); Henry van Dyke, *The Spirit of America* (1912); E. D. Adams, *The Power of Ideals in American History* (1913); and Bliss Perry, *The American Mind* (1912). Professor Perry has set a high standard for this type of work in *The American Spirit in Literature* (1918).

The statement with regard to the formation of the Connecticut Constitution in 1818 was derived from the illuminating monograph of Richard J Purcell, *Connecticut in Transition, 1775–1818* (1918).

CHAPTER VIII

THE JACKSONIAN ERA

THE administrations of Jackson and of his successor, Martin Van Buren, constitute a period of twelve years which may well be designated by any term which brings out the dominating personality of the President. The "Jacksonian epoch" and "The reign of Andrew Jackson" are frequently used; but the best description is contained in the phrase "Jacksonian Democracy," because it emphasizes the President's influence, and yet recognizes the other great element of the new Western democracy. It was partly a matter of temperament and personality, and partly a combination of circumstances that made the Jacksonian epoch a stormy period in American politics. The President personified the West of his time: lacking in education and refinement, but strong, energetic, and courageous. Untrained in administration, surrounded by a set of men who were themselves none too wise or experienced, unacquainted with and unappreciative of some of the larger phases of national development, it was inevitable that Jackson and Jacksonian democracy should come into conflict with the accepted way of doing things. The questions which came to an issue were more or less accidental.

Nullification The divergence of sectional interests led to one of the most dramatic incidents not only of this period but of all American history. The protective tariff of 1816 had been followed by others in 1824 and 1828, each carrying a substantial increase in the duties on imports, a result of the growing national feeling and nationalistic policy. Because of its manufactures the East was becoming more and more interested in the tariff and also in the establishment of improved communications with the West for the sake of opening markets, but was opposed to cheap land because laboring men were thereby drawn away. The West was in favor of a liberal land policy, cheap land, and internal improvements. The South, with its production of staple products, was opposed to tariff protection; it favored improved communications, but was opposed to Federal appropriations for that purpose, as it served to dispose of the unnecessary revenues accruing from the high tariff. As is usual in such cases, the South justified its opposition on constitutional grounds.

The manufacturing interests of the East and the planter interests of the South were thus opposed to one another and each was working for the support of the West. No section was strong enough to offset a combination of the other two. John C. Calhoun, as representative of the South, was attempting to form an alliance with the West by making concessions on the subject of greatest concern to that section, a more liberal land policy. In an effort to break the threatened alliance, Daniel Webster, senator from Massachusetts, attacked Robert Y. Hayne as champion of the South. This was the famous Webster-Hayne debate in 1830. It arose out of a discussion of a harmless enough resolution relating to the sale of public lands, at a time when the South was apparently making a deliberate bid for Western support, and it seems as if Webster, unable to meet that offer, like a skillful debater, shifted his ground and attacked the South at its weakest point, namely, on the assertion of State rights. He accordingly made his wonderful plea for a national interpretation of the Constitution. The course of events as well as the logic of the argument were on the side of Webster, although it may well be doubted whether Hayne was not historically in the right, that is to say, that he more nearly presented the interpretation of the Constitution as it would have prevailed at the time of its framing. But the forces of nationalism had brought the United States far beyond Hayne's position and it was for the Nation that Webster was speaking.

This debate occurring before Jackson had been in the presidency a year, an opportunity was made to test his sentiments on the subject. He was supposed to be a believer in State rights, whose sympathies were with the South; but he was also by nature a fighter and by training a military officer, who instinctively resented any effort to resist orders or to undermine central authority. When called upon at a banquet where nullification sentiments had been freely expressed, the President gave as his toast, in words which became historical, "Our Federal Union; It must be preserved!" The personality of the President had unexpectedly become a factor.

Jackson's unexpected opposition checked but did not stop the advocates of nullification. When the tariff of 1832 lowered duties but still maintained the principle of protection, the South felt that the time for action had come. In a convention composed in the same way as the convention which had ratified the Constitution of the United States, South Carolina adopted an Ordinance of Nullification, declaring the tariff of 1832 inoperative in that state. The President was aroused, Congress was called into the fight, and nullification was met by a threat of force, when Henry Clay relieved the situation by putting through the Compromise Tariff of 1833. South Carolina thereupon withdrew its Ordinance of Nullification, but issued another ordinance nullifying the Force Act, which was of no practical importance as there was now no need of putting it into operation. Victory was claimed by both sides, and with some reason for, after all, the result was a compromise; Federal authority had been maintained, but the tariff was changed.[1]

A few months later on a tour in New England, Jackson visited one of the towns in Massachusetts, where a manufacturing jeweler showed him cards and cards of buttons stamped with the palmetto tree. These had been ordered by the supporters of nullification and were to be worn as distinguishing badges, but they had been rendered worthless by the turn of events. "The President seemed greatly amused at the discovery that treason in South Carolina had its commercial value in Massachusetts."

The bank controversy The West had learned to fear a central financial institution and the dread of it was as potent then as was the Wall Street bogey fifty years later. Jackson shared the Western point of view and seemed ready to attack, but the

[1] It is interesting to note that almost at this same time an Indian controversy brought two of the Southern States into conflict with Federal authority, and in these cases, apparently because of his sympathy with State rights and his lack of sympathy with the Indians, Jackson upheld Alabama and Georgia in their refusal to abide by decisions of the Federal Supreme Court.

charter of the United States Bank would not
expire until 1836, long after the President's
term of office would have ended. To act under
such conditions was a delicate matter. It is
a pity to lose President Wilson's epigram that
"delicacy did not weigh with Jackson any more
than the judgments of the Supreme Court," [1]
but the responsibility must rest with Nicholas
Biddle, the president of the bank, and with
Henry Clay, who insisted upon bringing the
matter to a decision in 1832. A bill for the re-
newal of the charter was obtained from Congress, but Jackson vetoed it and made the bank
the issue of the presidential campaign of 1832.
Like every other difference of opinion this became a personal matter with the President,
and Jackson was a good fighter. When his
popularity brought him a triumphant reëlection, he promptly carried the war into the
enemy's country by ordering that no more
Government moneys should be deposited in
the national bank, but that instead they should
be distributed among various banking institutions throughout the country. This was in 1833
and the effects were far-reaching.

Railroads The generation of the War of 1812
had witnessed a complete change in
the character of American industrial develop-

[1] *Division and Reunion* (1893), p. 73.

ment. While still adjusting itself to the altered conditions another agency entered in which further stimulated the new development, but also produced some entirely unforeseen results. The steam locomotive was tried and proved successful.

The story of early railroading in the United States is not very different from that in other countries. As everywhere there were many amusing incidents connected with the first crude engines, track, and rolling stock. For example, a race on parallel tracks between a horse-car and a locomotive was won by the former. When two trains met on a single track, one was lifted off by the passengers to let the other go by. And nothing could picture conditions more vividly than the advertisement in Philadelphia that "The locomotive engine built by M. W. Baldwin of this city, will depart daily when the weather is fair, with a train of passengers' cars. On rainy days horses will be attached." There was the same, to us amazing, inability to appreciate the strength of the "force practically let loose suddenly upon mankind." The first railroads were expected to serve only as feeders for canals or as connecting links between water routes, and even then there was the inevitable opposition that accompanies every improvement. When the Boston and Albany Railroad was projected the *Boston Courier* said that it would be as "useless as a railroad from Boston to the moon," and a Dorchester town meeting declared that it would be of "incalculable evil to the town generally."[1]

Because of these things it is customary to consider the railroad as of little importance until a later time. While admitting the subsequent and greater usefulness, it will not do to ignore it in its beginnings. The mere fact that with twenty-three miles in 1830 there were nearly three thousand miles of railroad built in the United States before 1840, and that Congress in 1838 made every railroad a postal route, may not be overlooked. As a national force in binding together the various sections of the country the importance of the railroad was not yet felt, although the start was made.

Its immediate practical use was in transportation. Instead of the stage-coach pace of four to six miles, life begins to move at the rate of fifteen or twenty miles an hour. The railroad helped in further concentrating population in industrial centers, so that between 1820 and 1840 the city population increased more than twice as fast as did the population as a whole; but as an offset to this, one of its most im-

[1] Quoted by Howard Elliott, "Address to American Association of Traveling Passenger Agents," 1915.

portant effects in the United States was in assisting the spread of settlement.

Expansion New England population, as it expanded, had moved northward into New Hampshire and Vermont, and to some extent into Maine, and after the Revolution was over it had pushed out into western New York. For various reasons, about the time of the completion of the Erie Canal, large elements of that same population were ready to move on to the next stage. Some of the people had already gone and had settled the region within easy reach of the Great Lakes. If census maps showing the distribution of settlement are superimposed on maps indicating physical features, they reveal that the early comers into Indiana and Illinois took up land along the streams, and left the land between unoccupied; the toughness of the prairie sod made those stretches seem impossible of cultivation, and the question of transportation was a serious one. Gradually the pressure of population forced settlers slowly to encroach upon the prairie lands and, once the sod was broken, it was found that the soil was unusually fertile. Of course, as soon as a real demand came, a suitable implement was devised in the shape of a stronger plough.

Here, then, were great areas of land open to settlement, they were proving possible of cultivation, New Englanders were ready to come, and just at that time the railroad arrived. A few years later James Stirling wrote: —

There seems a natural pre-ordained fitness between the railway and the prairie; for the prairie is as eminently suited to the formation of railways, as railways are essential to the development of prairies. For hundreds of miles you have only to raise the turf, and lay your sleepers; . . . the prairies absolutely make their own railways without cost to any one. The development of the country by means of a railway is such, that what was yesterday waste land is to-day a valuable district. There is thus action and reaction; the railway improves the land; the improvement pays for the railway.[1]

It is little wonder, therefore, to find a rapid expansion of population into the prairie region of the Northwest, of which a large percentage came from New England by way of New York.

An additional reason for the westward movement of population was to be found in the increased pressure from foreign immigration. In the first forty years under the new government the total immigration was estimated at only 365,000, scarcely 9000 a year. But between 1830 and 1840 over half a million foreigners entered the country, more than 50,000 a year, and the total population of the United States was much less than 20,000,000. Of these immigrants 150,000 were German. Some of the newcomers went directly to the West;

[1] *Letters from the Slave States* (1856).

others remained in the East, forcing or making it possible for the native inhabitants to go West.

While the prairies were being settled in the Northwest the expansion of population into the Southwest had been continuing. Only there it was not so much a question of transportation as of opening new lands for cotton-growing. It must be evident what was happening: a stream of Southern settlers into the Southwest and a stream of Northerners into the Northwest forecast a division of the Mississippi Valley similar to that of the eastern seaboard. Before the situation, however, had sufficiently developed to become acute other things occurred of more immediate importance.

Public lands The steady movement of population into the West had brought insistent demands for modifications in the public land policy. The terms of sale as first arranged were probably unrivaled in the world, and yet they did not satisfy this people, which was, as Calhoun declared, "great and rapidly — I was about to say fearfully — growing!" Though the encouragement of settlement had not been left out of account, the primary purpose of the Land Ordinance of 1785 and the statutes which supplemented it was to obtain revenue. Accordingly the land had been offered in fairly large tracts. The West demanded that

land should be made more available for settlement and insisted upon lessening the amount
which might be sold to an individual, as well
as upon lowering the price. The process had
been gradual, but steady, until by an act of
1820 as small a plot as eighty acres could be
purchased at the price of $1.25 an acre.

There were few men who did not have or
could not obtain at least one hundred dollars
wherewith to buy eighty acres of land. If the
tract were in a desirable section its worth must
be greater than the price paid, and if it were
rich bottom-land, or if it were chosen for a
town site and laid out in town lots, its value
would be greatly enhanced. The one thing
needed was to realize on the valuation, either
by sale for cash or by obtaining credit. The
rise of manufacturing industries was accompanied by the growth of cities and of course
with an increased value of city lots. The opportunity for investment was unusual and the
chances for speculation were even greater. It
was at this particular moment that the President forced his attack on the United States
Bank by ordering the so-called "removal of
deposits," and the placing of Government
moneys in various state banks. These banks
doubled in number in the course of three or
four years. Some banks were established to
receive the Government deposits, some were

established for purposes of speculation, some were established honestly; but all issued paper money. This was the one thing needed to let loose speculation. Land which had been bought at a hundred dollars might be considered as worth ten times as much and would be used at one of the "pet banks" as security for such an amount. The fortunate individual immediately invested in still more land, which was in turn used as security for further borrowing. It was a time of boom towns, corner lots, speculation and extravagance. That the statement is not exaggerated is shown by the figures for the sale of land. Since the act of 1820 the sales had scarcely averaged in value two and a quarter million dollars a year. The "removal of deposits" began in 1833, and in 1835 the land sales had jumped to six times their former amount, while in 1836 the returns were only a trifle less than $25,000,000.

Panic of 1837 Only a moment's consideration is necessary to perceive that this was resulting in a vicious circle. The large amounts the Government was receiving from the sale of land were in the form of bank paper money. These receipts were in turn deposited with the various banks and became the basis of further inflation of the currency and expansion of credit. This could not continue indefinitely, and again it was the hand of

Jackson that precipitated the crisis. At this
time the revenues of the Government were
greater than its needs. The tariff of 1833 was
the result of a compromise to end the nullification controversy, and it was therefore considered inadvisable, if not a breach of faith,
to change it. For the first and only time in
its history there was an actual surplus in the
Federal Treasury which corresponded pretty
closely to the additional revenue from the increased sale of land. Something had to be done
with it; and as to give it to the states was believed by some to be unconstitutional, the
course suggested itself of making loans which
need not be recalled. Accordingly, in 1836, it
was agreed to distribute among the various
states the surplus of $36,000,000 in quarterly
installments, beginning in January, 1837. Unfortunately at this very time Jackson seemed
suddenly to realize the unsound condition of
the land speculation and ordered that all payments for land should be made in specie. Just
when the banks were being called upon to meet
the Government distribution of the surplus
and were accordingly under the necessity of
calling in their loans, not only were the specu-
lators forced to meet their obligations, but any
additional purchases of land had to be in specie
of which there was a marked shortage. The
bubble was pricked, the boom collapsed, and

the panic of 1837 was on. The Government made three of the quarterly payments to the states and then stopped, for it, too, was practically bankrupt.

The crisis of 1837 was severe, and as we look back upon it now its effects were startling. A reform of banking methods was a perfectly natural result, and it was the indirect consequences that were so striking. Believing in the greatness of their country's future, as well as caught in the mania of speculation, Americans had carried public improvements beyond the safety point. There was no justification, except that of enthusiasm, for the extent to which they were proposed. Capital in the United States was either insufficient or unwilling to finance the projects, and foreign capital had been induced to come in. To accomplish this the states stood back of the various enterprises. Sometimes the state itself undertook them, sometimes it guaranteed the stock, and sometimes it only subscribed as an indication of good faith. In going into the work of public improvements the states were discounting the future, borrowing largely and in some cases relying on their expectations of Federal Government support. From almost nothing state debts increased to over $200,000,000, and an equal amount was obtained from foreign investors. Then came the crash. Several of the states defaulted in payment of the interest and some actually repudiated the principal of their debts. It is no wonder that foreign critics were severe, that Sydney Smith should have written his pamphlet, *Letters on American Debts*, and that Charles Dickens, in *Martin Chuzzlewit* and *American Notes*, should have been so caustic in his comments on the American people.

These, however, were merely incidents of a financial crisis. What was of greater importance was the effect upon the Americans and the form their reaction took. They were inherently honest, and they were stung to the quick by the taunts that were cast at them. So sensitive were they, that a petition found its way into the halls of Congress that the debt of Mississippi, the first defaulting state, should be assumed by the Federal Government, and that Mississippi should then be ignominiously expelled from the Union. More practical, but perhaps no less radical, action was taken by most of the states themselves. In the period immediately following the crisis, provisions were inserted in various constitutions forbidding states to engage in the work of public improvements, or limiting the amount to which they might invest. Just at the moment when the state was in process of controlling, and in many cases of becoming the owner of public utilities, it was prevented from so doing. Private corporations had to step in and carry on the work.

Of almost equal importance was the effect upon the public land policy. The gradual shifting from the earlier emphasis upon revenue to an appreciation of the greater importance of encouraging settlement was hastened, until it might be said that the transformation was complete. It was as if the people asked themselves, "When the greatest profits ever known from the sale of land have proved to be worse than useless and have actually brought disaster to the country, why attempt to get any revenue from the land? Why not encourage settlement which would be for the benefit of the United States as a whole?" There is no doubt that from this time encouragement of settlement was the one great object of the Federal land policy. A significant manifestation of this is to be found in the fact that between 1840 and 1860 the Government disposed of some 270,000,000 acres, of which less than 70,000,000 were sold, the rest being given away.

Harriet Martineau was traveling in the United States when the craze for speculation was at its height, and in her *Society in America* she wrote: —

The possession of land is the aim of all actions, generally speaking, and the cure for all social evils, among men in the United States. If a man is disappointed in politics or love, he goes and buys land. If he disgraces himself, he betakes himself to a lot in the west. If the demand for any article of manufacture slackens, the operatives drop into the unsettled lands. If a citizen's neighbours rise above him in the towns, he betakes himself where he can be monarch of all he surveys. An artisan works, that he may die on land of his own. He is frugal, that he may enable his son to be a landowner. Farmers' daughters go into factories that they may clear off the mortgage from their fathers' farms; that they may be independent landowners again.

An interesting illustration of the change in public opinion is to be found in the matter of settling upon unsurveyed land. From the very outset the policy of the Government had been to insist upon survey of the land before sale or settlement would be permitted. Act after act was passed forbidding settlement upon unsurveyed tracts. The eagerness of the pioneers, however, was too much for them; men disregarded the law and took up lands in advance of the formal opening. Each time that a new act was passed, the Government allowed such "squatters" to hold the land upon payment of the regular price, but strictly forbade, under threat of severe penalties, similar action in the future. Such legislation could hardly be expected to be successful as a deterrent; the pioneers persisted and gradually forced their point of view upon the Nation at large. In response to this, Congress shifted its position and from time to time in the period under consideration passed general preëmption acts, practically offering a premium to the men who settled on the wild lands, and the Preëmption Act was made permanent in 1841. What had been a crime, or at least a misdemeanor, had grown to be a virtue.

In a way very similar to this the Government gradually changed its point of view on the subject of "internal improvements," or the building of improved communications at national expense. It will be remembered that when the Old National Road and the Erie Canal were built it was not considered within the province of the Federal Government to assist directly. But these highways proved too serviceable, especially in a new country, and the argument was promptly advanced that, if the Government did aid such undertakings, compensation would be had in the increased value of the public lands. And so when the rage for canal building swept the country after the successful completion of the Erie Canal, the pressure from the people, especially in the Northwest, was too strong. First the right of way through the public domain was given, with permission to use freely of materials for construction. Then, in the presidency of John Quincy Adams, who took a more liberal view of governmental powers, alternate sections of land on both sides of the right of way were given to the state to aid in the construction. Once adopted this method became the regular practice, first for canals and then for railroads, the principal change being that the amounts tended steadily to increase until the climax was reached in the granting of ten square miles on either side of the right of way, or twenty square miles for every mile of road that was built.

"Develop the country!" was the popular cry, and the uses to which the public domain was put met with hearty approval, that is, from Americans. Unprejudiced foreign observers saw serious evils in the American land policy. For example, Edward Gibbon Wakefield, the British authority of the period on colonization, pointed out the "evils of dispersion," arising from the scattering of population, declaring, "In the history of the world there is no example of a society at once dispersed and highly civilized."

It was Wakefield, also, who called attention to another consequence of the American policy. In 1836 a committee of the House of Commons was considering the subject of land in the British colonies and Wakefield was summoned as an expert. In answer to a question as to whether he considered the price of land in America sufficiently high, the witness made this startling assertion: —

I think decidedly not. . . . The value, to sell at market, of the slaves in the United States of America exceeds 120,000,000 pounds sterling. . . . It appears to me that if the price of land in the United States were high enough to provide for the combination of free labour, that is, high enough to compel every poor free man to labour during a certain term for wages, the slave population of the United States, instead of being worth 120,000,000 pounds to sell in the market, would become valueless. . . . My own opinion is . . . that the United States possess the means of abolishing slavery without injury to any one; and that those means reside in the price of waste land.[1]

Organized labor Such a striking bit of testimony reveals, as nothing else can, the significance of the fact, so wisely insisted upon by the late Professor Callender, that the real labor problem in the United States before the Civil War was — How to get labor. In the South it was solved by a compulsory system; in the North by establishing better laboring conditions than probably existed anywhere else at that time. In the latter section industrial changes were taking place so great as to amount almost to a revolution. But it was not merely "the domestication of the factory system" in the United States, with its great accompanying increase of so-called "laboring-men"; there were other forces also tend-

[1] This interesting and important item was brought to the attention of the author by Professor Payson J. Treat, of the Leland Stanford Junior University.

ing to bring working-men everywhere to a consciousness of their common interests. Unions
of separate trades were formed upon the basis
of a class interest common to them all.

This was practically contemporaneous with
the extension of manhood suffrage, and the
demands of enfranchised labor are significant.
With some of these we have become perfectly familiar, but others need to be recorded,
for without them a correct understanding of
the development of the United States is impossible, and this is especially the case with
the central feature of their programme. At a
meeting in Philadelphia, in 1839, of delegates
from twelve trade organizations their creed
was frankly put: "What argument can be adduced why a more equal distribution of wealth
should not be made?" Their answer to that
question lies at the foundation of American life:

We speak of a democratic republican education,
which regards all the children as equals, . . . to fit
them as members of society and component parts of
a free government; so when they shall arrive at
maturity, and are thrown upon the world and their
own resources, they may start equal in the race
for the accumulation of wealth, or in pursuit of the
honors of the government. This is the leveling system we desire — the only equal distribution of
wealth we ask.

Other forces were working in the same direction. Men who wanted to go into public life

187

were so completely dependent upon popular support that of necessity they did everything in their power to advance the cause of general education, so that the people might understand the appeals which were addressed to them. The most ardent advocates for the spread of education came from New England, and the religious motive for the support of common schools had largely disappeared. It has been well said that the industrial revolution which was taking place, together with the spread of democracy, caused a displacement of the political and social centers of gravity. It seems as if the former ruling class, finding their occupation gone, had sought some other outlet for their energies and had turned to philanthropy and reform.

Intellectual awakening An era of prosperity is usually accompanied or followed by an intellectual awakening as well as by philanthropic and humanitarian reforms. It is impossible to assign any exact dates for such a development, which is seldom instantaneous, yet it seems as if the Jacksonian era displayed greater activity in this direction than almost any other period. That a national spirit had been developing in literature was shown in the writings which were appearing in periodicals immediately after the War of 1812. The writers were apparently trying themselves out, and in the period under consideration a whole series of authors distinguished in American literature may be named: Bryant, Cooper, Emerson, Hawthorne, Poe, Whittier, Longfellow, Bancroft, and Holmes. Significant writings in the legal field were evidenced by Kent, Story, and Whiting; and in the economic world by Lieber and Carey. The first edition of the *Encyclopædia Americana* was published in 1829, and in these years Audubon and Asa Gray were making their contributions to natural science. In 1838 James Smithson endowed the Smithsonian Institution.

Reform But this was distinctly an era of reform. The General Assembly of the Presbyterian Church, in 1837–38, declared that "amusements and all parties the object of which is simply pleasure ought to be abandoned." This doubtless indicated concern over the spread of pleasure-seeking, but if this was to be restricted some outlet for the abounding energy of these people had to be found. Noticeable in this period, then, were the great missionary societies, home and foreign, and all sorts of religious organizations. Combe, in 1839, commented upon the charitable activities of the Americans and upon the large financial contributions that they made to these causes. He was describing the annual meetings of the benevolent and religious societies which were taking place in New York in the spring of that year, and after a brief account of the American Anti-Slavery Society, the American Tract Society, and the American Bible Society, he went on: —

The names of some of the other societies of which meetings are announced for this week, are the New York Marine Bible Society; the New York Female Moral Reform Society; the American Seamen's Friend Society; the New York and American Sunday School Union; the Foreign Evangelical Association; American Tract Society; American Moral Reform Society; New York City Temperance Society; American Board of Foreign Missions; New York Academy of Sacred Music.

There were various associations for prison reform and for more humane treatment of criminals. So much was done in the United States in the improvement of penitentiaries that the House of Commons, in 1834, ordered a report upon these institutions to be printed and distributed. A temperance wave swept over the Nation, leaving in its wake organized societies with over a million members. All sorts of communistic schemes were tried, so that one writer has made out a list of fifty-seven attempts to form "associations" between 1826 and 1846. There were organizations favoring the adoption of woman suffrage, for the suppression of lotteries, and for stopping the carrying of mail on the Sabbath. And

one of the many reforms was for the abolition
of slavery.

BIBLIOGRAPHY

J. S. Bassett has written the best *Life of Andrew Jackson*
(1911), although James Parton's *Life* (1866) still remains
authoritative because of its documentary material. The best
short history of the Jacksonian era is that of William Mac-
Donald, *Jacksonian Democracy* (1906). W. E. Dodd, *Expan.
sion and Conflict* (1915), is the latest good interpretation of
the period from Jackson through the Civil War, although
Woodrow Wilson's *Division and Reunion* (1909), referred to in
the text, cannot be neglected.

In addition to the volumes of the *American Statesmen* series,
previously referred to, attention might be drawn to Gaillard
Hunt, *Life of Calhoun* (1908), and to J. B. McMaster, *Daniel
Webster* (1902).

Important for their particular subjects are D. F. Houston,
A Critical Study of Nullification in South Carolina (1902);
R. G. Wellington, *The Political and Sectional Influence of the
Public Lands, 1828–1842* (1914); R. C. H. Catterall, *The
Second Bank of the United States* (1903); Lois K. Mathews,
Expansion of New England (1909); William Garrott Brown,
The Lower South in American History (1902); E. G. Bourne,
History of the Surplus Revenue of 1837 (1885); W. A. Scott,
Repudiation of State Debts (1893), and John R. Commons
et al., History of Labour in the United States (1918).

The Railroad forms a subject by itself, and the books upon
it are frequently gathered in special libraries. For the general
reader there is nothing better than F. A. Cleveland and F. W.
Powell, *Railroad Promotion and Capitalization in the United
States* (1909), while for the student E. R. Johnson and T. W.
Van Metre, *Principles of Railroad Transportation* (1916), and
B. H. Meyer (Editor), *History of Transportation in the United
States before 1860* (Carnegie Institution, 1917), are most useful.

CHAPTER IX

MANIFEST DESTINY

"DEVELOP the country!" had been the cry of the previous era, and to a large extent the energies of the people had been turned in that direction. Now, as a result of forces long at work the slogan became "Manifest destiny!" — which was understood to mean the occupation of the whole central portion of the North American continent and perhaps an even larger area.

Texas With the expansion of cotton-planting and the consequent desire for new land, the Southerners were looking with longing eyes toward Texas. As early as 1817, Peck's *Emigrant's Guide* had advised newcomers that there were wonderful opportunities in Texas for the growing of cotton, if permission to settle there could be obtained. For three centuries Spain had held that region, but without any particular interest in it. Missions were established, forts were built, and settlements were made; but only to guard against the aggressions of the French and later against the Americans. At the beginning of the nineteenth century the estimates indicate a white population in Texas of only one or two thousand. When Mexico revolted, along with other Spanish-American colonies, she was primarily concerned with maintaining her independence. Not being particularly interested in Texas, Mexico welcomed the opportunity to obtain the favor and support of Americans by opening that province to them. The Americans at once took advantage of what the Spanish and Mexicans had failed to appreciate for three hundred years. There may have been thirty-five hundred white people in Texas in 1821; within ten years they had increased to twenty thousand; while in five years more even those numbers had doubled, and practically all of the newcomers were Americans. They came mainly from the Southwest, they appreciated the advantages of the climate and soil offered by Texas, and there is no doubt that what they wanted was land where they could continue the pursuits in which they had been previously engaged, which was, to a large extent, the growing of cotton. There could be but one outcome of such a condition, the establishment of the independence of Texas, which took place in 1836, and then annexation to the United States.

Oregon Two streams of migration had come into the Mississippi Valley and two streams of migration flowed out farther into the West: the one into Texas as just noticed, and the other in the North to the Pacific Coast. It was not the later far-famed California that drew men to the coast, but Oregon. Trappers and fur-traders had visited the Far West and established their posts at various points, but the real movement for the occupation of the country came as the result of missionary enterprise. Neither Great Britain nor the United States had a superior claim to this northwestern region, and after the War of 1812, when many other matters were amicably arranged, the boundary line between Canada and the United States was continued as far as the Rocky Mountains and it was agreed that the country west of that should be open to joint occupation. The Northwest Company, and later the Hudson's Bay Company, was actually in control.

In the early thirties an appeal was made by the Flathead Indians for missionaries to be sent among them, which was taken up in Protestant pulpits, and coming as it did when the wave of philanthropy and reform was sweeping over the United States, the response was enthusiastic. The Methodists were first in the field, in 1834, and were promptly followed by Congregationalists and Presbyterians. As missionary ventures these efforts did not prove any too successful, but they succeeded in attracting attention to the Oregon country, and started a small colonization movement in that direction.

The Panic of 1837 had been followed by years of hard times on the frontier. The impulse of the frontiersman under such conditions was to move on, and it required only some added inducement to rouse him to action. In 1840 a bill was introduced in Congress which disregarded the agreement for joint occupation, and assuming the right of the United States to the Oregon country, recommended the building of a line of forts from the Missouri to the Columbia, and then proposed to offer 640 acres of land to every one who would go out and settle in the Columbia River Valley. Negotiations being under way for the settlement of the northeastern boundary between the United States and Canada, the Administration was afraid that this bill would be embarrassing. It was accordingly withdrawn, but when the Webster-Ashburton Treaty had been successfully concluded, in 1842, the bill was again introduced and was passed by the upper house. Early in 1843 Lord Palmerston declared in the House of Commons: " It is possible that the bill may not pass, but if it did pass, and become a law, and was acted on, it would be a declaration of war." The bill failed to pass the lower house, but the terms of the bill were known and widely published. The occupation of Oregon thereupon became a patriotic movement in which those who were animated by a spirit of adventure could engage, with the possibility of rendering a service to their country and at the same time benefiting themselves. Their patriotism was further stimulated by the desire to get ahead of the British. In consequence of this, in 1843, nearly a thousand people emigrated from the United States to Oregon; followed the next year by fourteen hundred more; and in 1845 there were some three thousand.

There was no use of Canadians or British trying to compete with such a showing, and a military commission sent out from London in 1845 advised their Government of that fact. The story is still current in Canada that the commission was made up of English country gentlemen who were fond of sport; reaching the Oregon country when the salmon were running in the Columbia River, they found to their disgust that the fish would not rise to a fly, and they accordingly reported that the country was not worth keeping. It is natural that the Canadians, as every other people in a similar position, should have felt from time to time that their local interests were sacrificed for what the British Government might consider the greater needs of the Empire. But with such a feeling existing it is easy to see how this particular story arose out of the simple fact that Lieutenants Warre and Vavasour, in order to keep their real mission a secret, outfitted in Montreal as sportsmen.

Politics The Oregon question, and Texas as well, now passed into American politics, where it was possible to make a party issue, as the various elements in opposition to "King Andrew" had united under the name of Whigs. Just as soon as the improved means of communication and transportation made such a method feasible, the party convention had been adopted as a regular piece of political machinery, offering a way of selecting nominees that insured a more general acquiescence in the choice. The financial disaster of Van Buren's administration contributed materially to the result, but whatever the causes, in the "log cabin and hard cider campaign" of 1840 — probably the most picturesque in American political history, a campaign of enthusiasm, "of monster meetings, carnival pomp, and doggerel verse" — the Whigs were successful in electing to the presidency General William Henry Harrison, a popular military hero of the West. Unfortunately, in an attempt to win Southern votes the Whigs had named as Vice-President, John Tyler, a Virginian aristocrat and state-rights Democrat who had split with Jackson. The choice proved to be disastrous, for Harrison died after being in office only a month, and Tyler, as his successor, could not work with the Whig leaders, so that the party lost strength. Just before the next presidential campaign of 1844, in an effort to regain favor, Tyler announced the conclusion of a treaty of annexation with Texas, which the Whig Senate promptly rejected, and for which even the House of Representatives showed its disapproval.

Henry Clay came out against the annexation of Texas and received the Whig nomination, while the Democrats for the first time made a "dark horse" their candidate, naming James K. Polk, a former congressman from Tennessee. It was a clever move on the part of the latter to choose catching phrases as party cries: "The Re-occupation of Oregon and the Re-annexation of Texas!" "The whole of Oregon or none!" "Fifty-four forty or fight!" Fearing that popular sentiment was against him, Clay tried to hedge on the Texas question, but he only lost votes thereby and Polk was elected. Thereupon the stipulated twelve months' notice was given to Great Britain, that the joint occupation of Oregon must terminate, and soon afterward in 1846, the question was amicably settled by treaty, the Canadian-American boundary line on the forty-ninth parallel being continued west of the Rocky Mountains to the Pacific.

The Mexican War While this was going on, namely in 1845, Texas also had been annexed. Although it was impossible to get a treaty to that effect approved by the necessary two-thirds vote in the Senate, the same result was accomplished through the adoption by Congress of a joint resolution providing for annexation, as this required only a majority vote of both houses. It was understood that this action, embodying as it did the acceptance of Texas claims with regard to boundaries, would result in war with Mexico. The President was an expansionist; he was determined to obtain California as well as these other additions, and he was therefore ready to go to war with Mexico and only wanted to justify the act. The reasons he gave in his war message to Congress of May 11, 1846, were that "war exists, and notwithstanding all our efforts to avoid it, exists by the act of Mexico itself," and that this was because "now, after reiterated menaces, Mexico has passed the boundary of the United States, has invaded our territory, and shed American blood upon the American soil."

Abraham Lincoln was elected to the next Congress. He was a Whig and therefore in opposition to the Administration, but he was also displaying that characteristic quality of his, which Kipling so aptly describes as the American ability to turn "Home, to the instant need of things," when he introduced into the House of Representatives a series of resolutions known as Lincoln's "Spot Resolutions." The substance of them was: "That the President of the United States be respectfully requested to inform this House . . . whether the spot on which the blood of our citizens was shed, as in his messages declared, was not within the territory of Spain," and later within the territory of Mexico; and finally, "Whether our citizens whose blood was shed, as in his messages declared, were or were not at that time armed officers and soldiers, sent into that settlement by the military order of the President, through the Secretary of War." These resolutions were never acted upon, serving merely as an introduction to a speech, but their import is unmistakable.

Early American interest in California had been largely a matter of obtaining furs and of trading on the coast. Only a few people from the United States had settled there, although some had gone from Oregon, and others who had started for the latter place had been deflected from their purpose by the superior attractions reported of California. But as the United States expanded, in its commerce as well as in settlement, a port upon the Pacific Coast became more and more desirable, and the interest of the Federal Government seems to have been primarily on that account. There are indications years before of an intention on the part of the United States to obtain California. It was hoped to acquire the province peaceably; but evidently instructions were given to the proper parties to take possession whenever the opportunity offered, and so as one of the campaigns of the Mexican War an expedition was sent to California, and the country fell easily into American hands.

After all, taking the various circumstances into account, it is not surprising that the United States went to war with Mexico. The astonishing thing is that once engaged in the war the Americans were content with so little. The result was a foregone conclusion, but with the unexpected success of the invading expeditions into Mexico, until even the impregnable Mexico City was in American hands, it is remarkable that the victors did not take all of Mexico. The sentiment in favor of it was stronger than might have been expected, and several of the Cabinet supported such a policy. However, the war had not been undertaken for this purpose; nor had there been time for the brilliant military victories to produce their full effects; and there was a growing feeling that this expansion would mean the extension of slavery. There is good history as well as good literature in James Russell Lowell's *Biglow Papers:* —

"Ez fer war, I call it murder, —
    There you hev it plain an' flat;
I don't want to go no furder
    Than my Testyment fer that;
God hez sed so plump an' fairly,
    It's ez long ez it is broad,
An' you've gut to git up airly
    Ef you want to take in God.

"They may talk o' Freedom's airy
    Tell they're pupple in the face, —
It's a grand gret cemetary
    Fer the barthrights of our race;
They jest want this Californy
    So's to lug new slave-states in
To abuse ye, an' to scorn ye,
    An' to plunder ye like sin."

And again, —

"Parson Wilbur he calls all these argimunts lies;
    Sez they're nothin' on airth but jest *fee, faw, fum,*
An' thet all this big talk of our destinies
    Is half on it ignorance, an' t' other half rum."

Peace was made with Mexico in 1848, and the United States not only assumed certain claims of its own citizens, but also gave to its defeated enemy $15,000,000 for the territories acquired. It is natural to regard such payment as a sop to uneasy consciences, and that may well have been one of the unconfessed motives; but it is rather characteristic of American generosity and fair play. Those, however, are matters of personal interpretation, and the facts are that by the terms of the treaty the title to Texas was placed beyond question and California was definitely ceded, together with the country lying between California and Texas; not that the Americans took any interest in the last region except that it rounded out their boundaries and protected their lines of communication. In less than four years the United States had increased its area by 390,000 square miles in Texas, 285,000 in Oregon, and 530,000 in the Mexican Cession, a total that was one third larger than the original area of the United States, and nearly equal to its area in 1840.

The Middle West Acquiring of vast territories was the conspicuous, but not the only phase of American expansion at this period. An increase of population from 17,000,000 in 1840 to 31,000,000 in 1860 (of which over 4,000,000 came through immigration), and the building of 27,000 miles of railroad, would necessitate a spread of population within the former boundaries. While the discovery of gold in California in 1848 caused a picturesque rush of adventurers and settlers to that region, an increase of a hundred thousand is almost nothing in comparison with a larger growth elsewhere. The less spectacular feature of American expansion, but the one of most importance, was the increase of settlement in the Mississippi Valley. Fostered by the liberal, or extravagant policy which sold land cheaply to any one and gave it freely to assist in the building of roads and canals, the Western population increased so rapidly that by 1860 many more than half of all the people in the United States were living beyond the Alleghenies. The center of wool-growing and the center of milling, as well as that of grain-growing, had also passed west of the mountains.

Industrial development
These were stirring years, when expansion to the Pacific appealed to the imagination of Americans, when the Mexican War aroused them (some, it is true, in opposition), and when the discovery of gold in California caused great excitement. Yet the mass of the people in the United States went about their ordinary occupations. It was unromantic, but from one point of view the most important aspect of the period was industrial, especially as many of the characteristic features of American industry seem to have become prominent at that time.

The great increase in railroad mileage already referred to was merely an indication of the extent to which improved transportation was being carried. So far as industrial development was concerned, a fundamental point was, of course, that steam transportation by land and by water permitted specialization to a much greater degree. It carried manufactured products to wider markets and it brought the necessary food and materials to the factory towns. By way of illustration, the use of coal instead of charcoal for smelting greatly increased iron production. By the new means of transportation coal might be carried to any point. But it was of greater economic importance that, when coal-fields and ore-beds were found together, the iron industry could concentrate there, relying upon the railroad to distribute its products and supply its needs.

Given these fundamental conditions, forces peculiarly American came into play, and the first of these was inventiveness. For some time after the cotton gin there seems to have been no great American invention, and then almost suddenly and in a comparatively short space there were invented or developed to the stage of utility the sewing machine, the McCormick reaper, the Goodyear process of hardening rubber, and the magnetic telegraph. And these were only a few of many, for the significant aspect of this American trait is that the United States developed a "democracy of small inventors." Until after the War of 1812 there were not one hundred patents a year taken out; in the period we are considering they increased to thousands. Local conditions were primarily responsible, but the ease of obtaining patents was a great encouragement, and as soon as the time was ripe development was rapid.

Automatic machinery was rapidly extended

through this inventive genius, because of the scarcity and high price of labor, but also because of the American's impatience with the mechanical repetition of a series of simple movements. Any device for the saving of time and labor received a cordial welcome. The inventor of the cotton gin, Eli Whitney, is credited with originating the system of interchangeable parts in the manufacture of firearms in New Haven, Connecticut, as early as 1800. It received an extraordinary impetus from its usefulness in machines for shoemaking and ready-made clothing. The sewing machine is an excellent example, and the use of such machines and of iron stoves seems to have led to the demand for interchangeable cast parts, until the combination of automatic machinery and interchangeable parts resulted in what was practically a new system of manufacturing, of which American firearms, clocks, and watches are typical.

Even this does not tell the whole story, for a series of obstacles was encountered in financing the undertakings on the scale required. There was not a sufficient accumulation of capital in the United States to make it easy to obtain the necessary funds for what were essentially speculative enterprises in trying out new inventions. The difficulty was met by the use of joint-stock companies, where the principle of limited liability permitted small investments by a large number of persons. Some were slow to accept the idea; for example, an act of the South Carolina Legislature on this subject was hailed by the *Greenville Mountaineer* as an act which should be entitled "An Act for legalizing fraud." [1] But states which refused to adopt the general principle, or which followed the British practice of requiring a special act and only after investigation had been made, found themselves so handicapped that the ultimate result was the passage of general incorporation laws. A British commission to the United States officially reported to their Government, in 1854, that "The Law of Limited Liability . . . is an important source of the prosperity which attends the industry of the United States."

In other countries developments such as have been described were slower in taking place and time was given for the necessary adjustment. In the United States everything happened at once; "All economic functions, banking, exchange, transportation, commerce, agriculture, manufactures, simultaneously adopted new machines and methods." America was still an agricultural commonwealth, but it was changing into an industrial state and the process was going on rapidly. In 1850 for the first

[1] Cited by C. S. Boucher, "Ante-Bellum Attitude of South Carolina," in *Washington University Studies*, III (1916), p. 252.

time the annual value of manufactures was recorded as surpassing that of agriculture, but by 1860 the priority of agriculture was reëstablished, the somewhat abnormal conditions having culminated in the financial panic of 1857. It is little wonder that there should have been some confusion, some irregularity, and some uncertainty, but the growth was vigorous, the country supported it, and came out of it crude and rough, but a country of great strength.

Prosperity As long as the United States could endure the strain of this great change and sudden development, prosperity was sure to result, and prosperity came. Some observers were impressed by "the absence of pauperism. Nothing is more striking than the universal appearance of respectability of all classes in America." Others were affected by the lavish use of the newly acquired wealth; the period has even been referred to as the "Golden Age." The high cost of living was charged up to the unnecessary sending parcels home by shop-keepers instead of the purchasers themselves carrying them as they used to do, and to the expense of decorations at entertainments. Such things are, after all, relative, and those who have lived long enough to experience an era of prosperity would recognize the following comments as characteristic, although these were made in 1857: —

From being once a domestic, quiet people, content to rest in their fireside comforts, and indoor society, — they are being all drawn abroad to seek for spectacles and public wonders! Now there are puffing advertisements to draw them abroad every night and day in the week — and this is not all — the whole must be indulged at so much expense! — One sees that it is working a serious evil; — but who knows how to stay it! To all this, add the rivalship of grandeur in houses — expensive furniture — immense and luxurious hotels — elegance and costs of Passenger vessels — and Passenger Cars — costly carriages — costly dresses for ladies and jewelry, — Pride and not comfort give favour to immense hotels, as some think.[1]

The same author quotes an interesting statement, presumably written about 1842, that is also thoroughly in keeping, regarding what is termed the "encroachments upon female modesty": —

Such came lately in the form of opera dancing, waltzing, and circus riding, wherein performers, in the display of limbs and individual symmetry, had the countenance of society.

Reform For the first time in contemporary accounts much was made of "the vile corruption of politics," the charge being, with the growth of a class of professional politicians and the great increase of wealth, that money was used improperly, both for bribing of voters and for accomplishing the miscarriage

[1] John F. Watson, *Annals of Philadelphia and Pennsylvania* (1857).

of justice. In such an atmosphere it seems as if the altruism of Americans must have been lost, and yet it manifested itself in various ways. There were many associations for the solution of social problems, while reform movements were even more extensive than those of the preceding decade, and it was to the people of that time that Emerson, the greatest of American idealists, made his successful appeal. Abolition was one of the *isms* being agitated, and though it was taboo in good society for many years, it eventually succeeded and thereby became one of the great reforms of the time.

Because it is so apposite as well as readable, it is ventured to use, even at the risk of too much quotation, an extract from the introduction to one of the volumes of the *Documentary History of American Industrial Society*, by Professor John R. Commons: —

The forties far outran the other periods in its unbounded loquacity. The columns of advertisements in a newspaper might announce for Monday night a meeting of the antislavery society; Tuesday night, the temperance society; Wednesday night, the graham bread society; Thursday night, a phrenological lecture; Friday night, an address against capital punishment; Saturday night, the "Association for Universal Reform." Then there were all the missionary societies, the woman's rights societies, the society for the diffusion of bloomers, the séances of the spiritualists, the "associationists," the land reformers — a medley of movements that found the week too short. A dozen colonies of idealists, like the Brook Farm philosophers, went off by themselves to solve the problem of social existence in a big family called a phalanx. The Mormons gathered themselves together to reconstitute the ten lost tribes. Robert Owen called a "world's convention" on short notice, where a dozen different "plans" of social reorganization — individualistic, communistic, incomprehensible — were submitted in all solemnity. It was the golden age of the talk-fest, the lyceum, and brotherhood of man — the "hot-air" period of American history.

BIBLIOGRAPHY

Several points in this chapter were developed from E. G. Bourne, *Essays in Historical Criticism*. G. P. Garrison, *Westward Extension* (1906), is the best single volume upon the expansion of this period, but gives proportionately too much space to Texas and the Mexican War in comparison with the acquisition of Oregon and California. There is no good history of the Pacific Coast, although H. H. Bancroft, *History of the Pacific States* (34 vols., 1882–1890), is the most voluminous and is useful and valuable for reference. T. H. Hittell, *History of California* (4 vols., 1886–1897), is much more useful for the average reader. Joseph Schafer, *History of the Pacific Northwest* (1905), is the best for that section. Josiah Royce, *California* (*American Commonwealths* series, 1886), is excellent, but only carries the history to 1856; and Stewart Edward White, *The Forty-Niners* (1918), is fascinating in its interest. George L. Rives, *United States and Mexico, 1821–1848* (2 vols., 1913), is the latest and best history of its subject. Upon the industrial development reference should be made again to V. S. Clark, *History of Manufactures in the United States, 1607–1860* (Carnegie Institution, 1916).

CHAPTER X

SLAVERY AND THE CIVIL WAR

THROUGH the persecution of the abolitionists, as well as from the continued agitation by them, slavery was gradually raised to the eminence of a moral issue, but it was not primarily in such light that it appeared to the people of the United States. To them it was almost entirely a matter of extending an undesirable institution into the newly opened territories in the West. It was thought that the Missouri Compromise, in 1820, had settled the question for all time, but that specifically applied to the "territory ceded by France to the United States, under the name of Louisiana." The recent territorial acquisitions had changed the situation, and it was a realization of that fact which had caused a large part of the opposition to the annexation of Texas and to the Mexican War. Northerners in Congress were sufficiently in the majority to have passed the "Wilmot Proviso," which would have prohibited slavery in territories acquired from Mexico, but owing apparently to a misunderstanding final action was not taken before Congress adjourned, and then it seems to have been hoped and assumed that the *status quo* in the newly acquired territories would be maintained.

Suddenly matters came to a crisis by the rush of settlers to California after the discovery of gold. If a territorial government had only been established, as was the right method of procedure, all might have been well. But Congress evaded the responsibility, largely because the two houses were unable to agree, and late in 1849 the settlers took matters into their own hands and set up a government for themselves. This was a characteristically American way of meeting the emergency, for which there were many precedents, and in this case the action would probably have met with hearty approval, if it had not been for the question of slavery. The gold-seekers established boundaries for their new state of California very much as they are at present, and they forbade slavery in the state thus formed. A glance at the map will show that a continuation of the Missouri Compromise line would have divided California into two parts. If it had been thus divided, it is altogether possible that the slavery question would not have been agitated at that time, and it furnishes an interesting speculation as to whether the Civil War might not have been avoided, for slavery would have been doomed before long through economic forces. The only warrant for what the

Californians did was the failure of Congress to act, which explains why John C. Calhoun could say that it was "a piece of gross impertinence," and indicates that there would be serious opposition.

The Compromise of 1850 Polk had been succeeded in the presidency by General Zachary Taylor, a military hero who was also a Southern Whig and a slaveholder. Straightforward to the point of bluntness, he favored the unconditional admission of California, and his assistance would probably have been sufficient to have carried the measure through Congress; but his unfortunate death occurred in the summer of 1850. Vice-President Millard Fillmore, who thereupon became President, favored the compromise measures of Henry Clay, which were ultimately adopted. This "Compromise of 1850," as it was called, provided for the admission of California as a free state; for organizing the rest of the territory acquired from Mexico without mention of slavery, leaving the inhabitants of each district to determine the question for themselves when they came to form a state; and for a new and more effective fugitive slave law.

The threatened rupture between North and South seemed once more to have been averted, and when one thinks of the manufacturing development taking place at that time and of the accompanying material prosperity, it does not seem astonishing that the people generally and business men in particular should have objected to anything that would disturb existing commercial relations between the sections. They talked and tried to convince themselves of the "finality of the Compromise of 1850." Oddly enough, at least at first thought, the situation seems to have strengthened political party organization. As slavery became more and more of a moral issue, men's consciences were growingly troubled and an excuse for inaction was welcomed. A man should stand by his party, and if the party determined that it could not take definite action on the slavery question, the individual was relieved and the responsibility placed upon the organization.

The Kansas-Nebraska Act But trouble was only temporarily avoided by the Compromise of 1850, and when it came again it was from an unexpected quarter. Stephen A. Douglas, United States Senator from Illinois, was a great believer in extending railway facilities throughout the West. He was a supporter of the Illinois Central Railroad, and without even insinuating the slightest unworthy interest on his part, he later would have been termed a "railroad senator." To advance the railroads farther into the West they must be built through the Indian country, the title to which had first to be extinguished and the land taken under Government control. This could be done by the creation of new territories, and Douglas accordingly introduced a bill for erecting the country just west of Missouri into the organized territories of Nebraska and Kansas. If there were any political motives involved, as commonly charged, they would seem to have been subordinate to the purpose of railroad extension. The area affected was partly within the boundaries of the old Louisiana Purchase, and partly within the territory acquired from Mexico. To objections from the South, Douglas conceded that in place of the Missouri Compromise the principles of the Compromise of 1850 should be in force. The Southerners pressed the advantage thus obtained, and in order to save the bill from defeat Douglas was forced to agree to the *repeal* of the Missouri Compromise. It was apparently a tactical necessity, but it proved to be a fatal blunder. At once the country was aroused.

The execution of the harsh and retroactive provisions of the Fugitive Slave Law stirred up bitter feeling in the North among the better people, while Mrs. Stowe's *Uncle Tom's Cabin*, with its overdrawn picture and exaggerated pathos, appealed to the masses especially when dramatized. It was wittily said that the Whig Party had expired in 1852 through an attempt to swallow the Fugitive Slave Act. Even with a Mexican War hero, General Winfield Scott, at the head of their ticket, the Whigs lost to the Democrats, who had chosen the good-natured and popular Franklin Pierce as their candidate. In that same year both Clay and Webster died, indicative of the fact that the old leaders were passing, and younger men were coming forward with demands for a new party which should not be afraid to meet the questions of the day. The Kansas-Nebraska Act furnished the issue, which was incisively stated in the course of the debate in Congress. Senator Badger of North Carolina had asked: —

Why, if some Southern gentleman wishes to take the nurse who takes charge of his little baby, or the old woman who nursed him in childhood, and whom he called "Mammy" until he returned from college, and perhaps afterwards too, and whom he wishes to take with him in his old age when he is moving into one of these new territories for the betterment of the fortunes of the whole family — why, in the name of God, should anybody prevent it?

To which Senator Wade of Ohio retorted: —

The senator entirely mistakes our position. We have not the least objection, and would oppose no obstacle to the senator's migrating to Kansas and taking his old "Mammy" along with him. We only insist that he shall not be empowered to *sell* her after taking her there.[1]

---

[1] James Ford Rhodes, *History of the United States*, I, pp. 452, 453.

Different parts of the country claim the honor of being the birthplace of the Republican Party, which would be of little importance if it did not show how general the movement was, and that the new party literally sprang into being. There were anti-Nebraska Whigs and anti-Nebraska Democrats; there were Know-Nothings and Free-Soilers; and even Abolitionists could support a party which opposed the extension of slavery into the territories.

The Kansas struggle
But the issue was not merely political. There was an actual physical contest for the possession of Kansas, which was foretold by William H. Seward, Senator from New York, when he cried: —

Come on, then, Gentlemen of the Slave States. Since there is no escaping your challenge, I accept it on behalf of freedom. We will engage in competition for the virgin soil of Kansas, and God give the victory to the side that is stronger in numbers as it is in the right.

In the North societies were organized to encourage and assist settlers, the most famous of which was the New England Emigrant Aid Company. This was unexpected, and was regarded by the South as not playing the game in accordance with the rules. On their part the Southerners were handicapped by the fact that their wealth was largely in land and slaves, but still they moved out in support of their cause, and we have the story of one owner chopping wood with his own hands for a fire to keep his slaves from freezing.

There is little doubt that the settlers from the North were the more numerous and that the Southerners won the first territorial election only by "colonizing" voters from Missouri. Believing that the territorial legislature had been captured by fraud, the anti-slavery men, without any other authorization than the conviction that they were in the majority, proceeded to set up an independent government, and to organize the territory as a state, which was of course to be a free state. Strictly and legally the Southerners were in the right until they should have been found otherwise by the courts. The free-state men considered themselves ethically in the right and being in the majority insisted that they were entitled to control the government. Under such circumstances, considering the time and place, fighting and bloodshed were inevitable.

Kansas was but typical of the whole struggle between the pro-slavery and anti-slavery forces. The Southerners were fighting a losing fight, held back by an economic system that most of the world had outgrown, and with a social life that in its finer phases had set many of the standards for American aristocracy, yet retained certain features that had been generally repudiated. Technically the Southerners were in the right; but potentially, because they were relying upon an institution that was inherently unfit, they were in the wrong. To maintain their position they naturally fell back upon legal processes. The Missouri Compromise was a favorite subject of attack because the mere differentiation of sections was an invidious discrimination, and since its adoption the South had been falling off in comparison with the North. The Compromise of 1850 had brought in a substitute, so far as the new territories were concerned, that was more acceptable to the Southerners, and also it had given them a fugitive slave law as stringent as they could wish and more severe than was wise. The Kansas-Nebraska Act repealed the Missouri Compromise; and finally, the Supreme Court, in 1857, was persuaded, in the Dred Scott case, to declare that the Missouri Compromise had been unconstitutional and was therefore null and void.

These were legal victories, but they were of no avail except to obscure the truth. The actual state of affairs was much better shown in a series of commercial conventions, beginning about 1845, which the Southerners called for the purpose of stimulating efforts to remedy their greatest weakness, their absolute dependence industrially upon the North. A speech that seems to have had a telling effect, for it was widely quoted and apparently repeated in different forms, revealed the situation: —

From the rattle with which the nurse tickles the ear of the child born in the South, to the shovel that covers the cold form of the dead, everything comes to us from the North. We rise from between sheets made in Northern looms and pillows of Northern feathers; we eat from Northern plates and dishes; our rooms are swept with Northern brooms; our gardens are dug with Northern spades; our bread kneaded in trays or dishes of Northern wood or tin; and the very wood with which we feed our fires is cut with Northern axes, helved with hickory brought from Connecticut and New York.

Election of 1860 For so young a party the Republicans made an excellent showing in the elections of 1856, and were able to secure a large number of seats in Congress; but for the highest office the young and not altogether trusted John C. Frémont was unsuccessful against the veteran Democratic politician, James Buchanan, of Pennsylvania. Under ordinary conditions Buchanan would probably have made a satisfactory record as President, but he was unequal to the crisis which was arising, and the country prepared for a change. In 1860 the Republicans outraged the feelings of the better men of the East by nominating the uncouth Abraham Lincoln from Illinois. There may have been clever political manipulation in the convention, yet it was Lincoln who in his marvelously direct way was already defining the issue between the North and the South more sharply than ever had been done before, and it was to this that the people responded in 1860. The Democrats were hopelessly divided between Northern and Southern factions, while other dissatisfied elements gathered under the non-committal name of the Constitutional Union Party. With four tickets in the field Lincoln obtained only two fifths of the popular vote, but he was supported by the most united organization and the votes of his opponents were so scattered that he succeeded in obtaining the majority of the electoral votes and was accordingly declared President.

With his sympathetic understanding of the Southern point of view, Woodrow Wilson has shown why Lincoln's election meant the parting of the ways: —

The Republicans wished, and meant, to check the extension of slavery; but no one of influence in their counsels dreamed of interfering with its existence in the States. They explicitly acknowledged that its existence there was perfectly constitutional. But the South made no such distinctions. It knew only that the party which was hotly intolerant of the whole body of southern institutions and interests had triumphed in the elections and was about to take possession of the government.[1]

[1] *Division and Reunion* (1893), p. 209.

Good fighters that they were, the Southerners took the aggressive, and acted promptly. Waiting only to be sure of the result of the election, a specially chosen convention in South Carolina unanimously adopted "An Ordinance to dissolve the union between the State of South Carolina and the other States united with her under the compact entitled 'The Constitution of the United States of America.'" Before the end of January, 1861, six other states from Georgia to Texas had passed similar ordinances of secession, and in the following month of February together they formed the Confederate States of America. Their constitution followed closely after that of the United States in the general framework of government, and the changes are mainly of interest because they so sturdily assert the Southern side of the sectional controversies of the preceding thirty years, including, of course, the protection of their cherished institution and of the principle of state rights.

The Civil War · It is idle to discuss whether the Civil War was fought on account of slavery or on account of secession. Theoretically, and so explicitly declared by Lincoln, the war was fought to preserve the Union. But secession, which had been an abstract right, was put into actual practice because of slavery. It is not too much to say that the

Southerners were sincerely actuated by high motives just as were the Northerners. In the assertion of their rights they believed that they were maintaining the principles of liberty which had been established in 1776, and it seems impossible to exaggerate either their devotion or the sacrifices they made in what is sometimes still referred to as "The Lost Cause." Nor is this inconsistent with recognizing, as in the days of the Revolution, underlying economic forces that seem to point to purely selfish motives. It was simply a case of self-protection. In an article in the *Atlantic Monthly* of January, 1861, James Russell Lowell wrote of the free states, that, in the eyes of the South, "Their crime is the census of 1860." [1]

If the war had been fought in 1830, at the time of the nullification controversy, it seems certain that the South would have won. War did not come then, and it was so long postponed because of the close commercial relations between the two sections — because of the concessions which Northern merchants insisted should be made to the South. Even in 1860 the two sides were after all not so unequal, for the South was a unit and many in the North were in sympathy with her, but at this point the West became the deciding factor. Sixty per

---

[1] Cited by J. F. Rhodes, *History of the United States since the Compromise of 1850*, III, p. 149.

POPULATION AND REPRESENTATION OF FREE AND SLAVE STATES, ACCORDING TO REPORTS OF UNITED STATES CENSUS

	FREE STATES			SLAVE STATES		
	Number	Total population (slave)	Representatives	Number	Total population (slave)	Representatives
1790	8	1,968,455 (40,370)	57	6	1,961,372 (657,527)	48
1800	8	2,684,621 (35,946)	76	8	2,607,223 (853,851)	65
1810	9	3,758,910 (27,510)	103	8	3,456,881 (1,158,459)	78
1820	12	5,152,372 (19,108)	123	12	4,452,780 (1,512,640)	90
1830	12	7,012,399 (3,568)	141	12	5,808,469 (1,999,356)	99
1840	13	9,728,922 (1,129)	135	13	7,290,719 (2,481,632)	88
1850	16	13,454,293 (236)	143	15	9,612,969 (3,200,364)	90
1860	18	18,726,007	147	15	11,464,290 (3,950,000)	90

Each state had two senators, but as long as the number of States was equal, the South had an advantage in the Senate because some of the Northern Senators could always be counted upon to support the Southern point of view.

cent of the people in the United States were living west of the Allegheny Mountains. The agricultural population of the Northwest had been in close relations with the South, but with the building of railroads the Northwest was finding an increasing unity of commercial interest with the Northeast. And that was only one element. The states and territories of the West were, or had been, colonies, and as such they were all creations of the Federal Government, so that their traditions were Federal and National rather than sectional. Most important of all, the people of the Northwest were generally anti-slavery in sentiment. So when the differences could no longer be compromised nor a decision avoided, the combination of all these forces brought the Northwest to the support of the Union and threw the balance overwhelmingly to the side of the North.

Contrary to appearances the Panic of 1857 was an ultimate misfortune to the South. Occasioned by speculation, over-expansion of bank credits, and too rapid investment in manufacturing establishments, the financial crisis produced its most serious effects in the Northern and Western States, while the great staple industry of the South was almost undisturbed. Cotton crops remained large, prices held firm, and although there were of course some consequences of the panic observable, in general the prosperity of the South continued. *DeBow's Review* declared: "The wealth of the South is permanent and real, that of the North fugitive and fictitious." [1] The unfortunate part of it was that Southern leaders were confirmed in their belief in the supremacy of cotton and went into the Civil War persuaded of the truth of their shibboleth "Cotton is King!" and convinced that the world was dependent upon them for its supply of this staple.

The South was disappointed in its failure to obtain foreign support, or even recognition, which might have materially affected the outcome. Great Britain angered the North by immediately according the status of belligerents to the Southerners, but the Federal leaders themselves were soon forced to take the same position, for they could not treat all Southerners as insurgents or traitors. Undoubtedly the British upper classes generally either sympathized with the South or were not loath to see the Union disrupted. Their attitude must have been influenced by the conviction that the South could not be subdued and therefore would ultimately succeed. This would explain the friendliness to the South in allowing the Florida and the more famous Alabama to be built in England and in permitting them to sail, while calmly ignoring the fact, which was

[1] Quoted by T. C. Smith, *Parties and Slavery*, p. 180.

patent to every one, that they were intended for the Confederate service. The British Government was later forced to acknowledge its fault and to pay heavily for its failure to live up to the obligations of neutrality.

Americans had always been irritated by the superior tone which the British had generally assumed toward them, and they resented it all the more hotly that American manners and culture, at least on the surface, bore out the criticisms that were made. The laxity, to put it mildly, of the British Government in the case of the Alabama was the culminating grievance and, as was prophesied at the time, aroused bitter feelings from which the friendly relations of the two countries suffered for over a generation. Nor was this bitterness alleviated by the fact that the great body of the British people, because of their opposition to slavery, favored the North, for Lincoln's specific declaration at the outset, that the war was not undertaken to abolish slavery but solely to maintain the Union, had bewildered and silenced the friends of the North. The way in which the operatives of the north of England bore the privation and suffering which came from cutting off the cotton supply was as significant as it was touching. When the inevitable happened and President Lincoln, as a war measure, late in 1862, issued his Proclamation of Emancipation, the tide of British public opinion, strengthened by Northern victories, turned steadily in favor of the Union and manifested itself more and more unmistakably.

It has been roughly estimated that the relative strength of the belligerent sections was as five to two, and odds as great as that were necessary. From the nature of the case it had to be aggressive warfare on the part of the North, and for years things went badly for that section; indeed, the outlook for the Union was not encouraging. Out of mistakes and disappointment, out of discouragement and even of defeat, emerged the soul of a man, melancholy to the point of gloom, but purified as by fire, so free from all thought of self, so resolute upon the saving of his country, and withal from so unpromising an exterior that all the world marveled. Great in his simplicity and simple in his greatness, humble in his power and invincible by his very humility, Abraham Lincoln held his people steady through the long period of trial. Time was required, but when the North finally found itself and put forth all of its strength there could be but one outcome.

It is claimed, and it might be admitted, at least at the outset, that Southern generals were superior to Northern generals, and Southern soldiers were the equals of Northern soldiers, for the Confederacy failed not because it was defeated in the field, but because it was starved and crushed into submission. The surrender of Lee to Grant at Appomattox in the early spring of 1865 was only the outward and visible sign of an inward collapse. In the absence of foreign intervention the North had been able to maintain and to extend its blockade of the Southern ports until finally the South was forced to yield. There were other causes, for the Confederacy within itself contained some disintegrating elements, yet it is safe to say that the North was finally victorious because of its superior resources. Might does not make right, but few could be found to say that the outcome of the Civil War should have been otherwise.

BIBLIOGRAPHY

With the Compromise of 1850 begins the scholarly *History of the United States* (7 vols., 1892–1906), by James Ford Rhodes. A. B. Hart, *Slavery and Abolition* (1906), presents the rise of the slavery question, and T. C. Smith, *Parties and Slavery* (1906), gives a good account of that aspect of the period just preceding the Civil War. Allen Johnson, in his excellent *Life of Stephen A. Douglas* (1908), hints at the railroad interest being the important element in the Kansas-Nebraska Act, and the subject is developed at length by Roy Gittinger in the *Mississippi Valley Historical Review*, March, 1917. Nicolay and Hay's *Abraham Lincoln: A History* (10 vols., 1890. Abridged, 1 vol., 1902), is the standard authority for Lincoln's life, although many shorter and useful biographies and sketches have been written. The recent one, by Lord Charnwood, is appreciative and most interesting.

The Civil War is another subject which has a literature of its own. Probably the best short account is that by J. F. Rhodes in a single volume, *History of the Civil War* (1917); F. L. Paxson, *The Civil War* (1911), is also good. John C.

Ropes, *Story of the Civil War* (continued by W. O. Livermore, 1895–1913), presents a careful and critical study of military events. Charles Francis Adams, *Trans-Atlantic Historical Solidarity* (Oxford Lectures, 1913), is excellent upon the relations with Great Britain.

The four volumes in the *Chronicles of America* series, Jesse Macy, *The Anti-Slavery Crusade*, William E. Dodd, *The Cotton Kingdom*, N. W. Stephenson, *Abraham Lincoln and the Union* and *The Day of the Confederacy*, with their different points of view, offer an unusual study in interpretation.

CHAPTER XI

RECONSTRUCTION AND ADJUSTMENT

WITH MALICE TOWARD NONE, WITH CHARITY FOR all, with firmness in the right, as God gives us to see the right, let us strive on to finish the work we are in; to bind up the nation's wounds; to care for him who shall have borne the battle, and for his widow, and his orphan, — to do all which may achieve and cherish a just and lasting peace among ourselves, and with all nations.

So closed on March 4, 1865, the second inaugural address of the President who was perhaps the only man who could have handled the delicate and difficult situation with which the United States was confronted at the close of the Civil War. Six weeks later Abraham Lincoln was dead at an assassin's hands, and the South mourned her loss, as did the rest of the nation and the world. His successor, the Vice-President, Andrew Johnson, was not equal to the emergency. As the years pass, recognizing his ability and his courage, history is doing greater justice to President Johnson than was formerly the case, but there is no disguising the fact that he was lacking in the very qualities which seemed to make Lincoln so fit for the task.

The negro problem The Southern problem after the war was a double one. Externally it involved the relation of the seceded states to the Union, while the internal problem was one of adjustment to new conditions. At its heart, in either case, lay the question of the negro as a citizen or as a laborer. The war losses, with which the present generation is becoming only too familiar, had to be repaired as speedily as possible. Naturally the Southerner returned to the only way he knew, that of the plantation and the growing of a few staple products, mainly cotton, the price of which in 1865 and 1866 had continued high. The plantation system, and practically the whole Southern organization, social and economic, had been based on negro labor in the form of slavery, which had been upset and demoralized by the war, and the negro generally was unreliable as a laborer except when he was made to work. Now, believing that the millennium had come, and misled by false promises on the part of designing men, too many of the former slaves relapsed into a hopeless state of idleness. Southern state legislatures, from industrial and social necessity, passed laws — the so-called "Black Codes" — which placed "persons of color" in a separate class, granting them ordinary civil rights, but discriminating

233

against them in other things, especially in connection with contracts for labor and in the matter of vagrancy. However justifiable from the Southern point of view and even from the actual condition of affairs, these laws were most impolitic, for to the Northern radicals it seemed as if the results of the war were being lost and that slavery was being reëstablished.

Thirteenth Amendment The situation was not improved after it became involved in politics. This had resulted primarily from the Thirteenth Amendment to the Constitution, abolishing slavery, which was a necessary corollary to the Proclamation of Emancipation, for the latter, as a war measure, had applied only to the states or parts of states specifically designated as "this day in rebellion." The amendment had been passed by Congress and submitted to the states in January, 1865; it was ratified and proclaimed in force in December of the same year. Inherently of the utmost importance, its political consequences were also far-reaching, because only three fifths of the slaves having been counted previously in apportioning representation, the abolition of slavery meant an increased number of representatives in Congress from the South. That section had been proceeding in the only direction in which it could see light by restoring to power the one group regarded as fit to control, the former governing class, the natural leaders of the South. The presidential policy of reconstruction, following the main lines laid down by Lincoln, tended to the same result. It was based on the belief that a loyal class existed in the Southern States which ought to be recognized and upon which it would be possible to rebuild the state governments. Although the policy was first carried out by the former opponents of secession, it had brought out more and more of the natural ruling class, many of whom were ex-Confederates. It was simply unthinkable to the Republicans, who had fought the Civil War through to victory, that these men should be allowed to come back with increased numbers to Congress, where they might by an alliance with the Northern Democrats dominate the national legislature.

The President and Congress The political complications are difficult to untangle, but some of the threads are conspicuous enough to follow, and one of these was the quarrel between the President and Congress. The two houses had early appointed a joint committee on reconstruction and, whether or not one approves of the specific measures taken, it would seem as if the members of Congress were instinctively right in opposing the overweening power of the President which had grown up in war times. Opposition to the excessive power of the executive was bound to arise, it would have come no matter who was in office, but it was unfortunate that the country did not have the benefit of Lincoln's firm and skillful hand and the advantage of his wisdom in this crisis. Senator Sherman said that the great defect in President Johnson's character was "his unreasoning pugnacity. In his high position he could have disregarded criticism, but this was not the habit of Johnson. When assailed he fought." This characteristic was never better exemplified than early in 1866, when the difficulties with Congress had begun. He was only responding to a serenade on Washington's Birthday, but in stating his own position on reconstruction, the President was unwise enough to charge certain members of Congress with being "I care not by what name you call them — still opposed to the Union." When asked to be more specific, he indiscreetly yielded: "Suppose I should name to you those whom I look upon as being opposed to the fundamental principles of this Government, and as now laboring to destroy them. I say Thaddeus Stevens, of Pennsylvania; I say Charles Sumner, of Massachusetts; I say Wendell Phillips, of Massachusetts."

Such utterances could do no good; instead of winning support they aroused antagonism;

and from that time the opposition was so far strengthened that it was able to muster a two-thirds majority in both houses of Congress, which made it possible to pass bills over the President's veto. The breach continued to widen and by the time Congress adjourned in the summer both sides were preparing for the approaching elections; it was a struggle for control of the new Congress. The President kept on in his unwise and undignified course by making a tour of the country which injured more than it helped his cause. Congress girded itself for the fray by establishing a campaign committee, which, under the name of the National Congressional Committee, became an important factor in the political party system, as it connected the central body more closely with local organizations. As a result of the elections the opposition to the President was entrenched in Congress more strongly than before.

The impeachment of the President Instead of yielding to the inevitable and recognizing the decision of the people, in so far as it was expressed in these elections, President Johnson persisted in keeping up the fight and Congress thereupon brought matters to an issue. The opposition almost invariably charges the President with improper use of patronage, and with that excuse, early in 1867,

Congress passed — over the executive veto as usual — the Tenure of Office Act, which required the consent of the Senate to removals from office. A few months later the Secretary of War, Edwin M. Stanton, refusing to resign upon request, the President dismissed him from office and, though the Senate withheld its consent, appointed a new Secretary of War. This was the opportunity for which Congress had been waiting and working. It was a dramatic moment in American history when the President of the United States, in 1868, was formally impeached by the House of Representatives and was brought to trial before the Senate. Eleven charges were preferred, although the only real indictment was disregard of the Tenure of Office Act. A two-thirds majority was required for conviction, but after all sorts of skillful maneuvering the prosecution was able to muster only thirty-five votes and there were nineteen for acquittal. A change of one vote would have found the President guilty.

The tendency at the present time is to regard the impeachment of the President as a mistake, even from the standpoint of partisan politics. Johnson may have been unfit to be President; he hardly was guilty of crime or misdemeanor. Great credit has been given to claimants for fame by the friends of one patriot or another, who is said to have cast the decisive vote which saved the country in this crisis. It is doubtful, however, whether that rightly presents the case. Many senators were willing to allow the matter to come to a trial, which was in itself a condemnation of Johnson's course; but at the last any one of several would probably have changed his vote so as to prevent the actual conviction of the President, which would have been regarded as a misfortune. Johnson was so thoroughly discredited, that General Grant had only to obtain the nomination of the Republican Party and his election was assured.

Reconstruction Even in such a summary of events one fact must stand out clearly, that in the years following the war Congress was increasingly the master of affairs. In that capacity it was responsible for the treatment which was accorded to the South, and though no one would now contend that the policy followed was altogether wise, it cannot be said to have been harsh, if looked at from the standpoint of victor and vanquished. The leaders in Congress were apparently actuated by a variety of motives in which vindictiveness was far outweighed by political policy and by a genuine interest in the welfare of the former slaves.

The Thirteenth Amendment had emancipated the slaves. The Fourteenth Amendment was designed to protect and to enfranchise them. After declaring that "All persons born or naturalized in the United States . . . are citizens of the United States and of the state wherein they reside," it provided that if a state should deny "the right to vote " to any citizens the proportion of that state's representation in Congress should be reduced accordingly. As a further safeguard, but with evident political purposes, former office-holders who had become Confederates were debarred from holding any office, state or federal, unless specially permitted by a two-thirds vote of Congress. The last clauses of the first section seem to be in keeping with the purpose of the amendment, but later they became one of the most effective weapons in the arsenal of corporations and so particular attention is called to them. The clauses read: —

No State shall make . . . any law which shall abridge the privileges or immunities of citizens of the United States; nor shall any State deprive any person of life, liberty or property, without due process of law; nor deny to any person within its jurisdiction the equal protection of the laws.

The immediate purposes of the amendment had been largely provided for in the Civil Rights Act and further supplementary legislation could if necessary have been enacted, but the efficacy of laws might be weakened and they might even be repealed, if Southerners or Democrats should come into power. A constitutional amendment was designed to put these things beyond the power of parties or states. The Fourteenth Amendment therefore became an essential part of the Congressional plan of reconstruction, and its adoption was made a *sine qua non* of admitting to Congress the senators or representatives of a seceded state. The refusal of the Southern States to ratify the Fourteenth Amendment, in which attitude they were encouraged by President Johnson, seemed to drive Congress into passing the supplementary reconstruction acts by which military governments were instituted in the Southern States. Under this system they were successfully "reconstructed" from the Congressional point of view, and the Fourteenth Amendment was duly accepted by 1868, but from the standpoint of the states themselves the method was most unfortunate. The former leaders being excluded, control passed into the hands of negroes and ignorant whites, and men came from other states to take advantage of this and to obtain for themselves positions of power. They were generally known as "carpet-baggers," but if they came from the South, and so were regarded as traitors to their own class, they were called "scalawags."

As may be imagined under such conditions the governments were incompetent and terribly corrupt. But the blame for this situation is not to be laid entirely on Congress or on the North. The Southern people were themselves intolerant and in some instances were guilty of outrageous conduct which led to extreme measures against them.

Even the provisions of the Fourteenth Amendment, to prevent withholding of the suffrage from negroes, proved ineffective and the Fifteenth Amendment was therefore proposed and adopted (1870), which concisely and specifically declared that the right of citizens to vote should not be "denied or abridged . . . on account of race, color, or previous condition of servitude." This met the requirements for the time being, but as the years passed it was becoming evident that the policy which the Government was carrying out was more or less of a mistake, and that it was wiser to leave control in the South to the Southerners themselves, for they could manage their own affairs much better than could the North.

General Grant remained President for eight years, and though he had supported Congress to a large extent, he had restrained that body from going to even greater extremes. The election of 1876 nearly rent the country in twain, so close was the contest for the presidency between the Democrat, Samuel J. Tilden, and the Republican, Rutherford B. Hayes. There are many who think, and with reason, that the Democrats won the election, but the returns were disputed and an ingenious and elaborate mechanism was devised for establishing an impartial commission to determine the result. The Republicans were in control of the Government, and in spite of all precautions the deciding vote in the Electoral Commission was Republican. The outcome was, therefore, pretty much of a foregone conclusion, and in order to keep the Democrats from adopting obstructive tactics in Congress, and so blocking a decision, the Republican leaders offered to withdraw the troops from the South. This was agreed to, Hayes was declared elected, and one of the first acts of his administration was the recall of the soldiers from the Southern States. The period of Reconstruction was over.

For years the whites maintained their supremacy by intimidation and actual violence until more peaceful methods were found just as effective. The late Senator Benjamin R. Tillman, of South Carolina, in a speech in 1900 was perfectly frank as to what had been done: —

You stood up there and insisted that we give these people a "free vote and a fair count." They had it for eight years, as long as the bayonets stood there. . . . We preferred to have a United States army officer rather than a government of carpet-baggers and thieves and scallywags and scoundrels who had stolen everything in sight and mortgaged posterity; who had run their felonious paws into the pockets of posterity by issuing bonds. When that happened we took the government away. We stuffed the ballot boxes. We shot them. We are not ashamed of it. With that system — force, tissue ballots, etc. — we got tired ourselves. So we had a constitutional convention, and we eliminated, as I said, all of the colored people whom we could under the Fourteenth and Fifteenth Amendments.[1]

The amendments were evaded and the negroes disfranchised by means of educational and property qualifications, and the whites who likewise would have been disqualified were exempted through the famous "grandfather clauses," by which any one could vote who had voted before 1867 or who was a son or a grandson of such a voter. Until very recently the courts, on one pretext or another, avoided rendering a decision in so delicate a matter.

Adjustment It is impossible to consider the history of the United States after the war without taking into account the facts that have been related, and yet the "reconstruction of the Southern States, though connected closely with the course of national

[1] C. A. Beard, *Contemporary American History*, p. 8.

politics, cannot be regarded as the foremost event, or series of events, in the period." The growth of the nation, the development of the United States into one of the greatest of industrial countries, and its recognition as a world power are the more important aspects of the last fifty years. In that process reconstruction was a retarding factor. The other side of the Southern story is constructive. Recovery after the war was the great and immediate need, and labor being essential, how to get it was the problem demanding solution. The difficulties which led to the passing of the "Black Codes" have already been referred to, with the unfortunate result of bringing about intervention by the North. When left to itself, too large a part of the negro working population tended to drift into the cities. As a labor class it was rendered still more restless and unsteady through competition and the paying of higher wages, that resulted from the great demand for labor, especially in Mississippi and Louisiana.

The New South   The planters had a hard lesson to learn, for it was contrary to everything they had been accustomed to, but they were meeting irresistible economic forces. By bitter experience they found either that they had to give up entirely, or that they must take labor on its own terms. Most negroes insisted upon becoming independent workmen; a few purchased their farms, some rented them, while others were content to work on shares; but the result was the same, the plantations were breaking up. Once it is appreciated that this meant the weakening of the foundation of the whole Southern social and industrial organization, other things seem insignificant, yet they cannot be ignored. Large numbers of whites, not accustomed to it, were obliged to go to work. The country merchant, rising to meet the needs of the small farms, became a relatively important person in the community. Small factories also grew up. These indicate one phase of the changes and development, while another was marked by an exposition at Atlanta in 1881. The South was waking up, and the Atlanta Exposition not only stimulated Southerners to new methods and new activities by exhibiting Northern tools and machinery, but it also revealed to an astonished North the industrial as well as the agricultural possibilities of the South. From that time on the industrialization of the South proceeded rapidly, a symptom of which might be found in the increasing attraction of foreign immigrants who had formerly shunned that section.

All of these things meant the creation of something practically unknown hitherto in the South, a middle class. It quickly revealed itself in educational demands, which displayed the ideal, so characteristically American, of better educational facilities available to all. There was the same ambition for advancement, the same insistence upon equal opportunity for all, that the workingmen's convention in Philadelphia had declared in 1839.

The point of view was taken earlier in this history that the United States remained in a position of colonial dependence for a long time after the Revolution, because foreign markets were essential. In the same way it might be said of the South that it remained a colonial section, dependent upon other sections and upon the world at large for marketing its surplus and for obtaining the products which it did not raise itself. The rest of the United States had broken its colonial bonds and had started on the path of nationalization two generations before, at the time of the War of 1812. The South had developed in its own way, but it had remained a province, — a splendid province, it is true, proud and aloof, yet an isolated section, a colonial dependency. Through a process of development, economic and industrial, through a social transformation and a changed attitude of mind, the South has grown into its rightful place in the Union. The New South is an integral part of the

United States; without it the country could never have achieved its present position, and the South is as proud of it as any other section.

CONSTITUTIONAL AMENDMENTS

The first ten amendments to the Constitution of the United States, declared to be in force in 1791, had been so closely connected with the adoption of that instrument by the several states, that they were regarded as a part of the original document. Although hundreds and thousands of other amendments had been proposed in various ways and at different times, down to 1865 only two had been adopted: one protecting a sovereign state from being sued by citizens of another state, and the other, after the controversy over the election of Jefferson in 1801, had simply specified that the electoral votes should be cast separately for President and for Vice-President. Now, within five years (1865–1870) three important amendments had been adopted. So difficult had it been before, and so difficult did it prove afterward, that it became a common saying that to amend the Constitution of the United States a civil war was necessary.

BIBLIOGRAPHY

J. F. Rhodes's work remains the standard history of the United States to 1877. Professor William A. Dunning, of Columbia, is the authority on reconstruction, and he has gathered about him a group of students, forming almost a school on this subject. Probably his own best statement is to be found in *Reconstruction, Political and Economic* (*American Nation* series, 1906). The newer point of view, that is on the constructive side, will be found in R. P. Brooks, *Agrarian Revolution in Georgia, 1865–1912* (1914), C. M. Thompson, *Reconstruction in Georgia, Economic, Social, Political, 1865–1872* (1915), and C. C. Pearson, *Readjuster Movement in Virginia* (1917).

RECONSTRUCTION AND ADJUSTMENT

Events in the United States since the Civil War have only recently been considered history rather than politics, and it is therefore difficult to recommend satisfactory historical reading matter. Quite the best account of the whole period from the Civil War to the present is that by F. J. Turner in the *Encyclopædia Britannica* (11th and last editions), and another good short account is that in F. L. Paxson, *The New Nation* (1915). A still shorter account is P. L. Haworth, *Reconstruction and Union* (1912). C. A. Beard, *Contemporary American History* (1914), is one of the volumes presenting a newer point of view. E. B. Andrews, *The History of the United States, 1875–1895* (1896, revised as *The United States in Our Time, 1870–1903*), is a readable account. The volumes in the *American Nation* series, of which Professor Dunning's has already been mentioned, include E. E. Sparks, *National Development* (1907), J. H. Latané, *America as a World Power* (1907), and D. R. Dewey, *National Problems* (1907). Ellis A Oberholtzer has begun a detailed *History of the United States since the Civil War*, but only the first volume has appeared (1917), carrying the narrative as far as 1868.

Several textbooks cover the subject in a fairly acceptable way, notably J. S. Bassett, *Short History of the United States* (1913), C. R. Fish, *Development of American Nationality* (1913), W. M. West, *American History and Government* (1913), and E. D. Fite, *History of the United States* (1916).

CHAPTER XII

THE GROWTH OF THE WEST

In sharpest contrast to the condition of the South during the war was the abounding prosperity of the North and the West. General E. B. Alexander, of the Confederacy, leaving his command immediately after Appomattox to sail from the port of New York, was dumfounded at the signs of universal prosperity and later remarked that, if the Southerners simply could have been escorted through the Northern States, the Civil War would have ended long before it did. They had believed that the North was suffering from the same privations which they were enduring.

It was inevitable that times should be hard at the beginning of the war, but it is surprising how quickly after the first shock the people of the North adapted themselves to the new situation. The well-being of a country so largely agricultural as the United States was necessarily dependent upon the farmers, and during the war not only were the crops good, but the harvests were large in spite of the shortage of labor, for farm machinery saved the work of many hands and women took the place of men who were at the front. Even with

the increased army demands there was more
than enough food for home use, and the surplus was exported at great profit. Other industries followed this lead and the accounts
of mining, of lumbering, of manufacturing, of
transportation, of everything, were but repe-
titions of the same story of growth and prosperity. That index of the working-man's state
and of general conditions as well, the savings
banks, showed "remarkable increases in the
number of depositors and amount of deposits." For those days the cost of the war was
fabulous, the debt incurred running up to some
three billions of dollars, and yet it was safely
financed.

**The Home-
stead Act** This was not the starting-point,
for the change had commenced
before the Civil War, but the
United States now proceeded rapidly onward in the career that ultimately
made it the leading industrial country of the
world. The greatest source of strength and
power lay in the West, and the development
of that section was hastened, oddly enough,
by the Civil War in altogether unexpected
ways. In the first place, the withdrawal of
the Southern members from Congress made it
possible to secure, in 1862, the adoption of the
Homestead Act in a form acceptable to the
President. By this act one hundred and sixty

acres of land were offered free to any citizen, or even to a prospective citizen, who would settle upon and cultivate the tract for five years. It was merely an extension of the previous land policy of the United States, but it marks the culmination of the use of the public domain for encouraging settlement. Under its terms approximately a million families have been provided for and it has been one of the greatest forces in later American development. Passed in the same year as the Homestead Act, and to be considered along with it, was the Morrill Act, which gave to the various states, for the development of agricultural and mechanical colleges, thirty thousand acres for every representative the state might have in Congress, and if any state did not possess the necessary public lands within its boundaries, an equivalent amount of land scrip was given.

A Pacific railroad Another way in which the Civil War rendered an unexpected service to the West was in the enactment of legislation for the building of a railroad to the Pacific. For years there had been no doubt as to the desirability of such a measure; the only question was one of location, and with the elimination of the Southerners the decision was easily reached in favor of the central route. In 1862 an act was passed making extensive grants for the Union Pacific Railroad, and although the name would imply, and many writers have asserted, that the justification of this act was found in maintaining and strengthening national bonds, the union referred to was that of different railroads, some of which were already in process of construction. By this act, for every mile of road that was built the Government offered ten square miles of the public land and a loan of sixteen thousand dollars in bonds. Two years later, when this had proved to be insufficient, the land grants were doubled and the bonding privileges greatly increased. Under the stimulus of such a reward the road was completed in 1869.

Important as was the railroad to the Pacific it should not be allowed to obscure the less spectacular but more generally serviceable railway extension that was being made elsewhere. The United States, as a country of magnificent distances, is utterly dependent upon means of transportation and it has been well said that America is essentially the child of the railroad. The period of recovery after the war was also a period of rapid expansion, and so great were the demands for transportation facilities that the country went mad upon the subject. Between 1865 and 1874 over thirty-five thousand miles of road were built, doubling the mileage that had been laid in the thirty-five years preceding.

Immigration
Opportunities existed in abundance if there was any one to take advantage of them, and the natural increase in population was not sufficient. The lack was partially supplied by incoming foreigners. Immigration between 1860 and 1870 amounted to 2,300,000 in spite of the Civil War, and in the following decade it increased to nearly 3,000,000. Over eighty per cent of these immigrants came from the northern countries of Europe, including Scandinavia and Great Britain, of whom at least a fourth and perhaps a third were Germans. It would be hard to overestimate the importance of immigration in the progress of the United States, as over four fifths of the newcomers were between fourteen and forty-five years of age, and so were reared at the expense of their home countries and came to America at the most productive period of their lives. The part they took in factory production is generally appreciated, but they were also of incalculable help in the development of the resources of the country, the exploiting of mines, the building of railroads, and the tilling of farms. In other words, they were an active force in the growth of the West.

The mining discoveries in the years after the Civil War attracted attention and drew the crowds as always, but the forces which have been described foretold an expansion of population of a different sort. All the elements being present settlement for a time was promoted on a scale never before witnessed. The offer of free land and the prospect of adequate transportation facilities, to a people increasing from twenty-five to thirty per cent every ten years, resulted not in settlement by individual families or small groups, but in colonization by wholesale. The story is a bewildering one, but no more confusing than the kaleidoscopic way in which the events themselves occurred.

The Indians
A first necessity in the development of the West was the termination of the Indian question. From earliest days the Federal Government had followed the policy, which it had inherited and accepted from the British, of keeping Indians and whites separated by a definite boundary line. When Louisiana was acquired the policy was only modified by removing the Indians to the Western country, where it was thought they would be isolated and where it was promised they might remain forever undisturbed. The futility of the promise was shown when expansion to the Pacific came. The beginning and end of Indian grievances was encroachment upon their lands by the whites. The only form of effective protest which they knew how to make was to fight, and the Indians took advan-

tage of the Civil War to protest vigorously and often.

Not long after becoming President, General Grant announced a new Indian policy, and coming from him it was unexpected, that it was cheaper to feed the Indians than to fight them. It is manifestly not possible to feed and clothe a tribe of Indians if its members are free to roam about wherever and whenever they please. The new policy, therefore, involved restricting the Indians to definite bounds, or, to put it plainly, it meant confining them on reservations. In the Indian Appropriation Act of 1871 a clause was inserted that "No Indian nation or tribe within the territory of the United States shall thereafter be acknowledged or recognized as an independent nation with whom the United States may contract by treaty." Independent Indian nationality had been a theory only and this declaration was simply a formal recognition of a condition long existing, but it nevertheless marks the beginning of the end.

The reservation policy inaugurated by President Grant would probably not have succeeded immediately or easily had it not been for the extermination of the bison, which had formerly spread in countless numbers over the whole North American continent, but were gradually restricted until in one great herd they occupied the region of the plains. The Union Pacific Railroad, completed in 1869, divided the bison into the northern and southern herds. According to the great authority on the subject, Mr. W. T. Hornaday, between 1872 and 1874 the whites killed over three million and the Indians over five hundred thousand of the southern herd; and the northern herd was exterminated in a similar way after the building of the Northern Pacific Railroad. Cutting off one of the greatest sources of their food-supply forced the Western Indians into submission, and reservations became the accepted arrangement. The last chapter of the pathetic story was written when good land became so scarce that the Indian reservations were broken up, on the pretext of giving each Indian a liberal amount of land for his own, but in reality that the balance might be thrown open to the whites. This was accomplished by the Dawes Indian Land in Severalty Act of 1887.

Cattle-ranching Where bison had thrived cattle were able to live. The industry was as old as the settlement of the continent, but in its modern form American cattle-raising had developed in the years before the Civil War on the great plains of northern Texas, where the cattle increased to millions. After the war the growing population of the West and the Government demand for feeding the Indians offered the markets that were wanted. The problem was one of transportation and delivery. When it was discovered that cows would fatten on the buffalo grass of the northern plains even better than in Texas, the problem was solved, and cattle-ranching spread rapidly northward over the western section of the United States and even into Canada. The cowboy became a synonym for the West. His picturesque trappings and engaging behavior, while making him a hero of fiction and the drama, diverted attention from the practical and serviceable work he was doing, but could not obscure the results. American cattle were exported to some extent, but the invention of refrigerator cars, by which in 1869 the first shipment was sent from Chicago to New York, not only revolutionized the slaughtering and meat-packing industry, it also carried American beef to all the world.

The romance of cattle-ranching has gone. Like so much else it has yielded to the progress of civilization. The old ways were too wasteful. A square mile of land for the grazing of every steer, which was a favorite method of calculation, was too extravagant when land was in demand and came to be at a premium. Intensive methods of feeding changed the average to a steer for every acre. The encroachments of the farmers broke up the cattle ranges.

Prairie farming All the elements were present and conditions ripe for an extraordinary agricultural development, and that was exactly what took place. The United States had long supplied its own needs, and now it exported its surplus products on a large scale and in increasing quantities until it achieved the leading place in the world's markets as a producer and exporter of breadstuffs and grains. But this involved changes that amounted almost to a revolution. In production it meant specialization to the extent of one-crop farming, and natural resources were supplemented by increased use of improved machinery. In distribution it meant classification and grading of grains; it meant the use of elevators for storing grain in bulk and the use of steam power in handling it. Finally the railroads provided the means of transportation, and the decline in rates made it possible to export at a profit. By way of illustration: for the decade ending in 1860 the exports of Indian corn, or maize, were something over fifty million bushels, while in 1880 they were nearly nine times as great; and for the same period the export of wheat rose from fifty-one to five hundred and fifty million bushels. Assuredly, prairie farming had justified itself.

BIBLIOGRAPHY

Among many books on such a variety of subjects it is difficult to select, but to the titles previously given may be added: E. D. Fite, *Social and Industrial Conditions in the North during the Civil War* (1910); C. F. Adams, *Railroads: their Origin and Problems* (1878; revised edition, 1893); the articles on immigration in the *Cyclopedia of American Government;* J. R. Commons, *Races and Immigrants in America;* F. J. Warne, *The Immigrant Invasion* (1913) and *Tide of Immigration* (1916); Emerson Hough, *The Story of the Cowboy* (1897) and *The Passing of the Frontier* (1918); and F. L. Paxson, *Last American Frontier* (1910).

CHAPTER XIII

A NATION AT WORK

To Americans it is so much a part of the natural order that anything different seems incomprehensible, but freedom of trade between the individual states of the Union has been one of the greatest agencies in their development and prosperity. So the growth of the West affected the whole country. Partly in the exploitation of new fields, partly in the production of raw materials, but mainly by its demands upon the other sections, especially after increasing its exports of grain, the West was in a large measure responsible for the next stage of industrial progress in the United States.

Diversity of manufactures For half a century factories of all kinds had been increasing, and with the variety and extent of America's natural resources, which meant cheap and apparently unlimited raw materials, it was inconceivable that manufactured goods should continue to be purchased to any great extent from abroad; it was only a question of time before the country should supply practically all of its own needs. The process of meeting the home demand was well under way before 1860; it was checked momentarily by the war, but was again furthered by the high war tariffs, and then continued uninterruptedly. From the standpoint of industry, among the most striking features of the years after the Civil War were increase in production and diversity in kinds of manufacturing, the result of the efforts to meet the requirements of home consumption.

It would be easy but profitless to go through a long list of manufactures reported in the official censuses so as to show the increase in and variety of production; the general trend is more clearly indicated by the simple statements: that between 1860 and 1880 the population of the United States increased about sixty per cent, while the growth in the value of manufactured goods was over three times as great; and that by 1870 less than seven per cent of the manufactured goods that were used came from abroad. If population increased at a fairly steady rate and if, as was the case, agriculture developed on about the same scale while manufacturing continued to grow several times as fast, there could be but one result. Until 1880 the United States was regarded as an agricultural country, because the annual value of the farm products was greater than that of manufactures, but by 1890 the balance had swung to the other side, and ten years later the value of manufactured products was dou-

ble that of agriculture. In 1894 the United
States attained the place of the leading manufacturing nation of the world. As soon as the
domestic demand was supplied the next step
was to enter foreign markets. The growth of
exports after 1880 is a commanding fact of
American economic history, and although
farm products continued to be the largest item,
manufactures furnished an increasing percentage until they became practically on a par.

The people of the United States therefore
changed from an agricultural to an industrial
population. In the days preceding the Civil
War, and for a time afterward, the dominant
interest in the United States had been that of
the farmers and the leadership had been taken
by the Southern planter. With the change
that had come, the controlling influence was
that of the manufacturer and the interests of
the planter and the farmer were necessarily
taking the second place. Professor Fish has
expressed the difference in a single sentence:
"The man who would rise out of the ordinary
in the 60's went into politics; in the 70's and
80's such a man went into business." [1]

The tariff A powerful stimulant to the manufacturing growth of the United
States was the tariff. It had been supposed

[1] Fish, C. R., *Development of American Nationality* (1913),
p. 460.

that, when finances were restored to more normal conditions after the war, taxes would be lowered. They were lowered, but only those which bore heavily on the productive resources of the country — in other words, the internal taxes. A corresponding diminution of import duties should have been made, but it was not, and the high war tariffs were continued. This was of enormous advantage to the manufacturers, but was expensive for the consumers, and in 1872 discontent was so great that Congress finally agreed to a general reduction of ten per cent in all tariff rates. This was an unscientific method of procedure, for it was not based on any analysis or even consideration of the subject; it was only a short cut in answer to the demand for tariff and revenue reform.

Panic of 1873 Over-production and over-trading, partly a result of the war tariffs, over-development of the West especially in the matter of railroad-building, and over-investment of capital were the real causes of a financial crisis, but they were aggravated by a fluctuating currency. The retirement of paper money after the war had stopped too soon to do away with the premium on gold. The usual characterization, that it was "brief, but sharp," would apply perfectly to the Panic of 1873, but the five years following were a period of declining markets and surplus goods, of idle mills and idle men, of strikes, lockouts, and bankruptcies. The reduction of the tariff had been only a minor cause, but it had to bear more than its share of the blame, and after the crisis had passed, without excitement and almost without comment, Congress restored the old tariff rates.

Corporations With the commercial failures accompanying the panic, partnerships and individual businesses were largely replaced by joint-stock corporations. So extensively was this resorted to, at the end of the five years of depression, that the period is sometimes referred to as the beginning of corporations in the United States. Such, of course, was not the case, for we have already seen how joint-stock companies with liability limited to the amount of stock subscriptions were made use of earlier and to a greater extent than in other countries. But such a statement at least calls attention to the great growth of corporations at that time, which was not merely for the protection of capital, but because of the extension of business and the increase of manufacturing concerns. The corporation, embodying the principles of limited liability, delegated management, and indirect ownership, offered a method of carrying on business on a large scale which proved so successful that it made this the preliminary period in the history of trusts.

There was something more in all these happenings after the Civil War than has yet been hinted at. Even the prosperity of the North could not hide the fact that the wastage of war had been enormous, and from sheer necessity the entire country was giving itself up to recovering the loss. The Panic of 1873 was a mere incident in a period of feverish activity. Other forces combined to bring the United States into one of the most dangerous epochs of its history. It was the inevitable reaction after fighting, when men returned from war after long years of brutality and of sordid life in the army, with illusions gone and, unfortunately, with many of their ideals gone, also. These men came back to find, too often, that the stay-at-homes had grown rich. There had been the ordinary irregular practices and a great deal of profiteering, whence arose the class of "shoddy millionaires," but even those who were actuated by patriotic motives and at the outbreak of the war had placed their factories at the Government's disposal were not at all averse to making profits and especially when the war continued so much longer than had been expected. It was a terrible misfortune for the United States in this critical time that many of those, who might have

led or at least restrained their generation, had
been among the first and best to respond to
their country's call and had been killed in
fighting. But whatever explanation is offered,
the fact remains that after the war the people
of the United States plunged into an orgy of
business and a wave of materialism swept over
the country such as it had never experienced before. For the first time, to any considerable extent, wealth became for Americans an object in
itself instead of being the emblem of success.

Concentration of industry
Of equal and perhaps greater importance, for economists say that
it is the striking feature of later
American development, was the
growing concentration of industry. Almost
any line of manufacturing could be chosen to
illustrate the fact that a smaller number of
establishments put out a greatly increased
amount of products. The localization of industry was usually a forerunner of concentration, and one of the earliest and most conspicuous instances was that of pork-packing along
the Ohio River, and especially at Cincinnati
after 1833, on account of the corn available
in the old Northwest, and because of the transportation facilities of the Ohio and Mississippi
Rivers. At about the time of the Civil War
the packing industry was shifted to Chicago
and the formation of the Union Stock Yards

in 1865 was the result of an agreement or an understanding between the leading pork-packers, and marks an important step in concentration and consolidation.

The railways furnish another illustration and seem to have set the example which many industries followed. Hundreds of roads, with a number of different gauges and an even greater variety in rolling stock, could exist only during a period of experimentation; self-interest in the direction of economy was slowly but surely producing its result. Even before the Civil War the process of amalgamation was under way, but Charles Francis Adams, one of the best railroad men of his time, chose the Saratoga Conference in 1874 as marking the change from the old order to the new, because of the effect it produced in getting the people accustomed to the idea of consolidation. Since that time the process has been rapid. As a further indication of what was taking place, Joseph Keppler, in 1881 with his cartoons in *Puck*, could pillory Jay Gould for the consolidation of the telegraph companies. A small group of men interested in the oil industry had come together in 1879 and in 1882 the Standard Oil Trust was formed.

Monopoly In his little book on *Railroad Transportation*, Mr. Hadley has sucessfully demonstrated that monopolies existed and were inevitable. It is not necessary to follow his arguments, for the facts, with which we have become only too familiar, speak for themselves. He was describing conditions as he saw them, and his work was published in 1885. The significance of this must be evident: the whole economic policy of the United States had been based on the principle of individual competition, and that principle was being undermined by forces which were irresistible.

The Fourteenth Amendment It was not accidental, therefore, that the early eighties saw an unexpected and to most people astonishing argument in behalf of corporations presented to the judicial courts. In pleading the San Mateo County case (1882), ex-Senator Roscoe Conkling, who had been a member of the Congressional Committee on Reconstruction, declared that the Fourteenth Amendment, which was supposed to have been adopted for the benefit of the negroes, had also been intended to protect other interests "appealing for congressional and administrative protection against invidious and discriminating state and local taxes." The journal of the committee seemed to bear out the claim, and when the matter finally came up for decision by the Supreme Court of the United States in the Santa Clara County case in 1886,

Mr. Chief Justice Waite, in a preliminary announcement said: —

The Court does not wish to hear argument on the question whether the provision in the Fourteenth Amendment to the Constitution, which forbids a State to deny to any person within its jurisdiction the equal protection of the laws, applies to these corporations. We are all of the opinion that it does.

This marks an important development in American constitutional as well as industrial history. The Fourteenth Amendment thereby took its place alongside of "the most important clause in the Constitution" which gave Congress power "To regulate Commerce . . . among the several States." Under these two provisions every conceivable sort of case has been carried into the courts. The Fourteenth Amendment was adopted in order to bring the protection of the Constitution to the enfranchised negroes of the South. Among the cases which have come up under it are: —

A suit to recover the value of a dog in Louisiana on which no tax had been paid; the right of a preacher to hold meetings on Boston Common; the right of a woman lawyer of the District of Columbia to practise before the courts of Virginia; a suit in New York to recover damages for the illegal use of the plaintiff's photograph; the sale of cigarettes in Tennessee; the regulation of the height of buildings in Boston; the question whether a convicted murderer in Idaho should be hanged by the

sheriff or by the warden; the question of the sanity
of a certain man in Alabama; . . . determining the
amount of damages for a dog bite in Michigan; . . .
reducing street-car fares for school children in
Boston; the labeling of mixed paints in North
Dakota; the selling of game in New York; . . . the
right of women to vote in Missouri; and the regulation of graveyards in California! . . . Yet these
are but a small number of cases selected at random.[1]

When it is appreciated that every sort of
subject could be brought within the scope of
the Fourteenth Amendment, and that a corporation was a "person" in the eyes of the
court, only one thing more is necessary to
understanding the value of this to corporations
or rather to selfish business interests. Until
very recently changed by federal statute, when
a state court declared a state law invalid
because it was in conflict with the federal Constitution or with a federal statute, there was
no appeal to the Supreme Court of the United
States. It was only when the local decision
was against the federal instrument that appeals
could go to the federal courts. Accordingly
the Fourteenth Amendment meant in each
state what the highest court of that state
wanted it to mean, and hundreds of laws were
nullified by the action of state courts. Professor Edward S. Corwin is quoted as saying

[1] Collins, C. W., *The Fourteenth Amendment and the States*
(1912), pp. 31–33.

that "'due process of law' is not a regular concept at all, but merely a roving commission to judges to sink whatever legislative craft may appear to them, from the standpoint of vested interests, to be of a piratical tendency."

In *Lochner* vs. *New York* (1905) the Supreme Court declared a New York law null and void because it limited work in bake-shops to ten hours a day, and the right to contract with regard to hours of labor was a part of the "liberty" protected by the Fourteenth Amendment. In dissenting from the decision Mr. Justice Holmes protested that the Fourteenth Amendment did not "enact Mr. Herbert Spencer's *Social Statics*." It was the freedom, one might say the recklessness, with which the courts nullified laws that was largely responsible for the growth of popular feeling against the judiciary and led to a demand for the recall of judges.

The labor question As we look back after thirty years' experience and see industry growing and concentrating even to the extent of monopoly, and realize that American institutions had been shaped with protection of property and encouragement of capital as primary objects, it is easy to understand why trouble with labor was inevitable. The local organization of separate trades in the United States dates back to the end of the eighteenth century, and though unions of different trades were established as early as 1827, their activities had been rather a part of the humanitarian movement, and they became of greater national importance only after the Civil War, especially with the organization of the Knights of Labor. The Panic of 1873 was accompanied with the usual hard times and wage reductions and was followed by the usual strikes, which in this instance revealed the growing strength of the labor organizations.

A fundamental cause of the difficulty between labor and capital was that America had always been noted for the high pay which labor could command. Wages both real and nominal had tended to increase rapidly, and in the period between 1860 and 1880 they were said to have risen over forty per cent. The greater benefits labor received, the more intelligent it became, the greater power it achieved and the greater the share it demanded as its right. The employer, on the other hand, was resentful because he considered the working-men ungrateful when they were better paid than anywhere else in the world. Such was the situation when the concentration of industry is observable in the early eighties. The importance of labor is shown by the creation of a Commissioner of Labor under the

Department of the Interior in 1884, and it is not accidental that the Knights of Labor numbered nearly three quarters of a million members in 1886, nor that that year showed a new high-water mark in strikes.

Immigration As manufacturing developed to the point where the United States became a factor in the world's markets, that is, when the export of manufactures became an important feature, the necessity for economy in production arose. A natural step for employers to take under such circumstances was to bring immigrants from different parts of the world in an effort to obtain cheaper labor. Professor Commons has well said that the competition between races is a competition in standards of living, and in the search for cheaper labor in the United States "the ends of the earth have been ransacked." A variety of races also made organization of workmen more difficult; where many languages and dialects were spoken, a union on a common basis was long impossible; and employers were unquestionably following such a policy deliberately.

The change in the character of immigration to America is noticeable after 1880, as there was a marked falling off in the proportion of those coming from the northern countries of Europe and a corresponding increase of those from other lands. In the decade before 1880 immigration had amounted to nearly three millions and was considered astonishingly large, yet in the next decade it increased to over five millions, and between 1900 and 1910 it jumped to over eight and a quarter millions. By 1907 previous percentages were almost exactly reversed: less than seventeen per cent of the incoming foreigners were from Germany, Scandinavia, and Great Britain, and over seventy-five per cent were coming from Italy, Austria, Russia, and Poland.

The great industrial problem of the United States in its earlier years had been one of production and from that standpoint, as previously noticed, immigration was of enormous assistance, for the difficulty had been how to get labor and not how to treat it. But a new problem was arising. The policy of the United States had been based on the principle of individual competition. With the breaking-down of competition came increasing fortunes for captains of industry, while the relatively low wages maintained through rivalry of races meant that a comparatively small share went to labor. The new problem with which the United States came face to face, really for the first time, was the distribution of profits and of wealth.

BIBLIOGRAPHY

E. L. Bogart, *Economic History of the United States*, is the best general sketch of the subject, but special works must be used to supplement on particular topics. Among the most useful of these are: C. F. Adams, *Railroads: their Origin and Problems* (1878; revised edition, 1893); A. T. Hadley, *Railroad Transportation, its History and its Laws* (first printed in 1885, but several subsequent editions have appeared); C. W. Collins, *The Fourteenth Amendment and the States* (1912); Hannis Taylor, *Origin and Growth of the American Constitution* (1911); William Z. Ripley, editor, *Trusts, Pools and Corporations* (1905); John R. Commons *et al.*, *History of Labour in the United States* (2 vols., 1918); and F. J. Warne, *The Immigrant Invasion* (1913).

CHAPTER XIV

BUSINESS AND POLITICS

THE Republican Party after the Civil War was very different from what it had been originally. Such varied elements and factions and classes had combined with the primary purpose of winning the war that in the election of 1864 the party had called itself "Union." But later, as it emerged with new leaders and with new policies, it went back to the old name to which clung the prestige of the claim that the Republican Party had fought and won the war, and therewith preserved the Union. Loyalty and patriotism were thus called in to strengthen party allegiance and enthusiasm. The war also affected politics through the acceptance of military standards, of subordination to leaders, of implicit obedience, and with little inclination to question methods provided quick action and speedy results were achieved.

The party machine   Party organization had existed before, with a system of committees, conventions, and delegates, but it was clumsy, and only under the new conditions did it get to "working like a machine" and to running so smoothly that "machine" became the name that was commonly applied. Political theorists have been inclined to attach considerable importance to the organization of a Congressional Campaign Committee to help win the elections of 1866 in the fight with President Johnson. Through this committee, which was made up of one member from each state, local politics and the local machine were linked up with the national party organization. Serviceable as this may have been in uniting separated elements, it would seem as if a more important agency had been the steady improvement in means of communication coming from railroads, the telegraph, and newspapers, so that all sections of the country and all localities were kept in close touch with one another, making it possible to fit the pieces of the party machinery together. An equally important factor was in the disorganization of the old party system before and after, as well as during, the Civil War owing to external conditions, and in new powers getting control. It was as inevitable as the corporation and it was in a sense modeled thereafter. Efficiency in politics was obtained by organization and one-man power, just as it was in the business world.

The rise of the boss system in politics was closely connected with the material growth of the United States. Business could adjust itself to almost any conditions, but it desired those conditions to remain stable and it relied upon the Government to maintain them. Sometimes more direct favors were asked for, but whatever was wanted business demanded results. The boss system made for efficiency, and one-man power was easier for business to deal with. Indeed, the boss was an almost inevitable phase in the existence of a class of professional politicians, and the system was not established by any sudden stroke, but so gradually that it was unperceived. Before they had grown to arrogance and pride of power, the men who were running the machine tried to find out what their constituents wanted, and they were successful politicians who met those demands so far as was possible and without friction.

The dominance of the Senate The bosses began, of course, in the smaller local organizations, but with the growth and spread of the system they were soon entering Congress from where they could control affairs almost as well as they could at home and where they had greater influence and power. But while this was in process of evolution another important modification in the national legislative body was disclosing itself. This was in the astonishing power, amounting to domination, exercised by the Senate. The upper house, in its stability through a longer term of

279

office, by its approval being required both in appointments and for the ratification of treaties, and by its dignity as the highest court of impeachment, possessed the attributes of a superior body. In other words, the stage was ready, but the events were more or less accidental that brought the Senate into the leading rôle.

The struggle with President Johnson happened to take a form in which the success of Congress was to the great advantage of the upper house, for the Tenure of Office Act placed removals from office at the discretion of the Senate. Inasmuch as the consent of that body was necessary before the original appointment could be made, it is easy to see that, if united action could be obtained, the Senate might control appointments absolutely. It was here that the smaller senatorial body, rendering concerted action possible, probably developed its most important consequences. In the years before the Civil War, it had been the practice for congressional delegates to suggest and to a certain extent to dictate appointments to federal offices within their states. This now hardened into the custom of the "courtesy of the Senate," which meant that the upper house would refuse to ratify an appointment unless approved by the senators from the state in which the appointment was made. It was virtually making "the President a mere clerk to transmit nominations handed him unofficially by the individual senators."

The House of Representatives as a body gained nothing in comparison with this, and we observe the unusual condition, especially in a republic, of the power of the upper house increasing when in most countries it was being reduced. During Grant's administration, owing partly to the inexperience of the President in matters of civil government, senators were able to exert their influence to the extent of imposing upon him their point of view and, except in isolated instances, they were rarely thwarted by Grant's successors. In commenting upon the difference in the practice of recent years, Senator Hoar, in his *Autobiography*, said that when he had gone into Congress "the Senators went to the White House to give advice to the President, not to take advice from him."

The method of manipulation to produce results is of little consequence. The dominant Speaker and his Committee on Rules in the House, and a Committee on Committees which served as a "steering committee" in the Senate, are merely incidental: "A small inner circle was formed in each house of Congress which ruled the party as an ordinary boss rules the machine." The caucus was the meeting of the members of a legislative body who were of the same political faith, and it has been well said that while it was the highest expression of majority rule, it was servile to the commands of party leaders, shut out publicity and responsibility, and opened the way for corruption and sinister influences. The more important feature is that, with the development of party organization and with the control of patronage, the Senate became the head of the political machine. It had the whip hand over the House of Representatives, for, if the members of the latter body wished to obtain a share of the spoils, they must submit to the senators who controlled the political appointments in their districts. The Senate accordingly became the desirable abiding-place for the state bosses or for those who were acceptable to them. One of our sanest writers on political subjects could recently assert that "Pennsylvania is preëminently the state of a boss"; and that its "political history for the last fifty years has been the history of its senators."[1]

Republicans in power
The Senate was the controlling organ of the Government and the Republicans were the controlling party in the Senate. In fifty years after the outbreak of the Civil War there was

[1] Jesse Macy, in *Cyclopedia of American Government* (1914). II, pp. 636, 637.

a Republican majority in the Senate four fifths of the time. During two thirds of that period the Republicans also controlled the House of Representatives, and the only Democratic President was Grover Cleveland, who was twice elected, in 1884 and 1892. James A. Garfield was chosen in 1880 to succeed President Hayes, but was foully assassinated a few months after entering office, and his place was taken by the Vice-President, Chester A. Arthur. Then came Cleveland, and between his two terms Benjamin Harrison was President from 1889 to 1893. After Cleveland's second term was finished, in 1897, the Republican succession was unbroken until President Wilson's election in 1912. In this long period of ascendancy the Republican Party was responsible for the organization, such as it was, of the federal finances; it was answerable for the maintenance of the war tariffs, until a high tariff had become the normal order; and business had grown accustomed to these things. Business corporations wanted the support of Government; the Republicans were the party in power and wanted the support of business; and so the two drew together naturally and almost unconsciously. The Republican Party, which originated in the West as a party of revolt against the complaisance of the established order, which had won its way to political power essentially as a party of the people, and which had fought the Civil War as a national party, gradually shifted over until it became the party of business interests. It was the party of bankers and manufacturers of the cities of the East, rather than the party of the agricultural states of the West.

Business in politics Corruption of law-makers was no new thing, for whenever a legislative body had something of worth in its gift, a purchaser was apt to be found. We have seen that the adoption of the Ordinance of 1787 was not above suspicion. When the first United States Bank expired in 1811, state bank charters became of value, and in New York, as a special act of incorporation was required in each case, bribery of the legislature became the accepted method of obtaining a charter. The building of the Pennsylvania Highway, beginning with the Act of 1827, was accompanied by irregular and corrupt practices, quite in the modern style, and a legislative committee in 1841 reported "that within the period of a single year, by the policy and practices which have prevailed, the public money, to a large amount, has been squandered and improperly paid away." [1]

[1] Quoted by Avard L. Bishop, *The State Works of Pennsylvania* (1907), p. 235.

The principal difference in the later conditions was that they invited temptation. Better means of communication were so important for Americans that improvement and transportation companies were a favorite form of investment, or of speculation. Railroads were so much wanted that it was the custom not merely to permit their companies to organize, but to encourage them by granting special favors. When many companies grew rich, or at least made money for the promoters, lobbying to obtain special franchises became the ordinary method of procedure. There is but one outcome to such a situation; it may begin with irregular practices, it is sure to result in direct bribery.

In the decade before the Civil War one finds many references to corruption in politics, and they become more frequent in the years after the war. This might be attributed to the widespread materialism of the time, but the better explanation lies in the frenzy for expansion and development which led to excessive railroad-building and in the alliance of business and politics. The railroads were the head and front of the offending, or rather they set the pace which the others followed. Their officials seemed to be the first to have become imbued with the idea that they were a privileged class because they were rendering a service to the people, and it grew into a spirit of arrogance, unless it was bravado that led them frankly to show their attitude and to reveal their practices. If the railroads were the teachers, big business was an apt pupil and soon surpassed its master.

The development that has been sketched could not take place without being appreciated more or less clearly throughout the country. When the disclosures of the Tweed Ring scandals in New York were made in 1871, the people seem to have been shocked not so much by the fact of the corruption as by the character and extent of the "graft." Even then it was regarded rather as a local affair, although the revelation that a Wall Street broker dared to go upon Tweed's bail bond seemed to point to a sinister alliance between business and politics. To future historians or interpreters of events it may prove of almost equal significance that the *New York Times* found it was good journalism and profitable to expose the whole sordid affair.

Liberal Republicans Nor could the development be appreciated without arousing considerable opposition. The Liberal Republicans in 1872 started the first of the third-party movements after the Civil War, and while it arose immediately out of dissatisfaction with the reconstruction policy, it gathered up a variety of discontented elements and included those who were opposed to the tariff and those who were suspicious of the general and widespread corruption. There was a chance for the success of this reform movement until the mistake was made of placing the enthusiastic and well-intentioned but erratic reformer, Horace Greeley, at the head of the ticket; when Grant, with his great personal popularity, was easily reëlected.

Discontent Corruption was only one of the forces making for discontent. The exploitation of the country's resources by individuals, who may not have been so much favored as they were far-sighted or lucky, and the promotion of manufacturing in a country which had been agricultural would seem inevitably to work hardship upon the former predominant class, the farmers, and the earliest manifestations of dissatisfaction appeared in the agricultural states of the West. Although not rising as yet to the dignity of an independent political party, the Granger movement in the West was significant for the future. The farmers were looking to Government for relief. They were inclined to ascribe their troubles to a large extent to the railroads, and to make those organizations the central point of their attack. In a series of so-called Granger Laws, which were passed by several of

the Western States about 1873, a direct effort
was made to regulate rates and by the establishment of commissions to control ware-
houses and shipping facilities. Owing to the
panic and its effects, these laws were never
given a fair trial and they were in most cases
subsequently repealed, but a new doctrine
had been promulgated in the United States,
and was upheld by the Supreme Court in *Munn*
vs. *the State of Illinois* (1877), that railroads
were public utilities and as such amenable
to state control. The Granger movement in
politics subsided for a time, yet its reforms
and ideas became of importance in later years,
for the tide of discontent was not checked,
but was rising and swelling.

Reform Another phase of the growing dissatisfaction was expressed in the
Civil Service Reform movement. A common
method of raising political funds for meeting
party expenses had been by the assessment of
office-holders. The party organization being
generally held responsible for existing conditions, it seemed as if the best measure for
breaking it up was to take away its financial
support. If merit were substituted for party
service as the basis of appointment, and if
assessments were cut off, it might be possible
to destroy the machine. There always had
been men working for the betterment of the

civil service, and the agitation for reform was of early origin, but something more was necessary to arouse the mass of the people. The presidential election of 1880 was significant for the efforts of the Republican machine to control the national convention. A compelling motive, therefore, was found in the growing antagonism to the political machine, and an immediate cause for action came in 1881 through President Garfield's assassination by a disappointed office-seeker. Even then it is doubtful if the politicians would have acted had it not been for the congressional elections of 1882, which resulted in a great Democratic victory and pointed to a similar result in the choice of a President two years later. The Republicans were ready to run to cover and, as civil service reform would prevent partisan removals, just before losing control of the House, in 1883, they passed the Pendleton Act, which still stands as the basis of the reformed civil service of the United States.

To the surprise and disgust of its supporters, the Pendleton Act did not achieve anything approaching what had been expected of it. The reform spread and ultimately succeeded in improving the service to an extent almost unbelievable, when the conditions before its adoption are considered; but progress was so slow, especially at the start, that it seemed as if nothing worth while had been accomplished. The more disappointing aspect was that the reform failed in one of its chief purposes, that of weakening the political machine by forbidding the party assessment of federal office-holders. It is impossible to run a machine without oil; and when their regular supply was cut off the party managers turned to another source, from which they had previously received some aid. They applied to large business corporations, which were ready and even glad to contribute, but of course expected a return. Party finances were more easily and more generously supplied than ever.

This cemented the union between business and politics; and business was non-partisan. "Where the treasure is, there will the heart be also." Perhaps business favored the Republican Party somewhat because of its principles and policies, but the Republicans were supported primarily because they were the party in power. "The statement of a railroad magnate, that in Republican counties he was a Republican, and in Democratic counties he was a Democrat, but that everywhere he was for the railroad, was the cynical admission of an attitude easily understood."[1] It might be better to say that business was bi-partisan, for that is the form which the political organiza-

[1] Seth Low, *The Trend of the Century*, p. 20.

tion took in many of the state legislatures, a combination acting through corrupt leaders of both parties irrespective of party affiliations.

Business and the Senate With bosses in Congress, with the overweening power of the Senate, and with the alliance between business and politics, it should be clear why and how the representatives of big business went into the Senate in their own persons or saw to it, upon agreement with the party bosses, that the men sent were sure to be favorable to business interests. There is no more striking illustration of the power of the Senate and of the way in which it was used to favor special interests, than is to be found in the making of tariff laws. By the Constitution, which embodied the British tradition, the lower house as representative of the people was given sole power to initiate revenue bills, but the upper house was not prevented from amending and, with its superior organization and power, the privilege of amendment was carried to undreamed-of lengths. To a measure which came from the House hundreds and hundreds of amendments might be made, or an entirely new bill might be substituted for it. When the differences were finally referred to a conference committee of the two houses, the senatorial members almost invariably won out. The manipulation of tariff legislation of recent years, which is common knowledge, is justly laid at the door of the Senate.

Australian ballot   When civil service reform failed to break the political machine, which only became more arrogant and more corrupt with its increased funds, another remedy was sought in changing the method of voting. Bribery at elections obtained and was believed to be even more widespread than the facts seem to warrant, so that while the actual use of money in the election of 1888 was bad enough, the stories of it grew into a scandal. Claiming that, if the ballot were secret and men were free to vote in accordance with their convictions, bribery would be vain, the Australian ballot became the panacea. First adopted in Massachusetts, after the election of 1888, it spread like wildfire and was in force in most of the states within a very few years. Again the reformers were disappointed, and there is even ground for claiming that the Australian ballot strengthened party organization. Certain it is that the party machine was quick to seize the advantage. In grouping the candidates under party names and symbols in order to place all parties on a footing of equality, legal recognition was given to the party organization, which had never been accorded to it before.

The politicians were able men, in general far shrewder than the reformers, and quickly adjusted themselves to new conditions. Long before the "good citizen" even thought of the danger, the boss had ingratiated himself with the newly arrived immigrants, and in their ignorance was able to swing their votes at his will. Each reform had taken years of agitation before adoption and years of trial afterward. Each had accomplished something, but had fallen far short of perfection. It is surprising that the people still retained faith in any remedies, but hope springs eternal and every new plan was able to rally ardent supporters. To the thoughtful observer, however, it was evident that the root of the trouble had not been found and that something more radical or something entirely different was necessary.

BIBLIOGRAPHY

Bryce's *American Commonwealth* is in a class by itself as describing political conditions in the ⊔nited States prior to the appearance of the first edition in 1८.॰॰ subsequent editions have not improved it in this respect. ⊔⊔e character of Professor Jesse Macy's work has already been referred to in the text, and his articles in the *Cyclopedia of American Government* are especially to be commended. More connected accounts will be found in his *Political Parties in the United States, 1846–1861* (1900), and *Party Organization and Machinery* (1904). Other books on this subject which have already been referred to are M. I. Ostrogorski, *Democracy and the Party System in the United States* (1910), H. J. Ford, *Rise and Growth of American Politics* (1898), and A. T. Hadley, *Undercurrents in American Politics* (1915). Books to be recommended upon their special subjects are S. J. Buck, *The Granger Move-*

ment (1913), F. E. Haynes, *Third Party Movements* (1916), and C. R. Fish, *The Civil Service and the Patronage* (1905).

Among the useful memoirs of the period are: J. G. Blaine, *Twenty Years of Congress* (2 vols., 1884–1886); Carl Schurz, *Reminiscences* (3 vols., 1907–1908); Hugh McCulloch *Men and Measures of Half a Century* (1888); G. F. Hoar, *Autobiography of Seventy Years* (2 vols., 1903); and John Sherman, *Recollections of Forty Years* (1894).

CHAPTER XV

THE SECOND GENERATION

THE progress of the United States, ordinarily running smoothly and steadily onward, has been occasionally interrupted; its course may have been retarded or it may have been stimulated, the regularity of the flow was broken. Oftentimes the interruption was but momentary or of little consequence, and only rarely has it been of great importance. The most striking instance of the latter sort was observed at the time of the War of 1812, and now there came a similar extraordinary period about 1890. The forces at work were many, corresponding to the complexity of modern life, and if traced out one by one each seems to show a fairly normal activity with only a slight acceleration at the time mentioned. Yet the sum of all the changes resulting shows a total so large as to warrant considering the second generation after the Civil War the most important period in the history of the United States since the generation after the Revolution. Perhaps an important agency is found in the phrase just used, which is taken as the title for this chapter, that the generation of the Civil War was passing and another generation was coming on the stage with new purposes and fresh ideas.

American idealism Prosperity undoubtedly had much to do with the new order, for prosperity meant that more and more Americans were free from the everlasting drive of merely making a living, and that leisure and opportunity were given for other things. The rise of sport, the adoption of baseball as the national game, and the increasing enjoyment in being out of doors gave a wholesome turn to their point of view, and it might well be claimed that the regenerating force in American life was the introduction of the "safety bicycle" from England in 1885, especially with its widespread popularity through the invention of the pneumatic tire in 1888. These were controlling factors in setting the standards and in moulding the ideals of the new generation. A strain of practicality had manifested itself in 1815 and it is doubtless true that the materialism of the period after the Civil War influenced somewhat the ideals that were taking shape, and yet they were thoroughly in keeping with American character. Sensitive, artistic minds, especially of other nations, sometimes sneer at those ideals as materialistic, and perhaps they are. But they do not seem so to Americans who recognize their practical cast, for the essence of their idealism is service to mankind. And American scholars keep step with their countrymen: "Not truth for truth's sake, but truth for life's sake," is their creed.

In other respects also the Americans of this era bred true to type and never more so than in the matter of education. Compulsory schooling for all of younger years is a necessary step in raising the level of the masses and is hardly a distinguishing feature. The conspicuous thing in the American system is the continuance of the higher stages of education at public expense, even to the university and in research, and the opening of those opportunities to practically every one who will take advantage of them. The working-men's demands of 1839 have been realized beyond their wildest dreams.

It would be possible to show a similar development in almost every phase of American life: The Columbian Exposition at Chicago in 1893 revealed unexpected possibilities in the field of civic architecture, and also indicated a deeper appreciation among the people of all things artistic; it was the day of yellow journalism, as well as of an awakening in literature; heresy trials in the churches proclaimed the revolt against outworn creeds, for the demand was insistent that the needs of the time should be met, and fresh enthusiasm was aroused for every scheme of social betterment. These instances are chosen at random and they were but outward manifestations, themselves only slightly affecting the direction in which events were turning; the compelling cause lay deeper. If there be any value in the sketch of American development that has been attempted in this book, it must lie in the recognition that a great variety of forces produced the modern American and in the presentation of elements sometimes neglected. A careful survey of these and of others in this particular period leads to the conclusion that in most respects conditions were normal, that progress was uniform, and that the unusual is to be found in connection with free land.

The end of free land For years the Commissioners of the Land Office in their annual reports had been calling attention to the decrease in the public domain and to a threatened shortage of desirable lands. The shocking extravagance which had characterized the whole public land policy, with its exploitation of natural resources, had been accompanied by criminal waste and fraudulent abuse of land privileges by cattlemen, by lumbermen, and by corporations, especially railroads. The Dawes Act of 1887, which permitted the break-up of the Indian reservations in order to open to white settlement whatever land was left over, discloses the condition. The growing scarcity of available land focused attention upon the subject and coincided with far-sighted scientific projects for reclamation of the arid lands and for preservation of the forests. An irrigation survey was begun in 1888. The previous year a Division of Forestry was established in the Department of the Interior, and the first Forest Reserve was made in 1891. Conservation had begun. In his address as President of the American Historical Association in 1910, Professor Turner pointed to the significance of this change in policy, that it meant a conversion from "the ideal of individual freedom to compete unrestrictedly for the resources of a continent" to the ideal of restricting individual competition for the benefit of society. In his earlier article on the frontier, Turner had taken the census announcement of 1890, that it would no longer include a frontier line on its population maps, as the basis for his declaration that "the frontier has gone, and with it has closed the first period of American history."

An agency that had been active from earliest colonial times and regarded by many as the greatest force in American history was losing its strength. The coincidence of this with the climax of industrial development in the direction of monopoly must be apparent, and it is so significant that one wonders why it was not better appreciated at the time. The free land, which for over two hundred and fifty years had served as a refuge for the discontented, was being cut off at the very time when industries were concentrating and labor was reacting against monopolistic tendencies. The slackening of one would inevitably allow other factors to work with greater potency and every observable change may be accounted for. It was not accidental that immigration from Canada to the United States reached its culmination in 1890 and then turned the other way, so that before long the United States was "furnishing annually a larger proportion of the total number of emigrants into Canada than any other country."

The Populists The reasons for widespread discontent are obvious; some sort of reaction or revolt was sure to follow, and looking back, with the advantage of nearly thirty years' perspective, it seems inevitable that it should have arisen in the West. The immediate cause was the usual one of over-expansion and over-development. Shortage of other lands and a succession of rainy years had tempted settlers, especially in Kansas and Nebraska, to take up farms beyond the safety line of annual rainfall. When the dry years came, as come they must, crops failed, mortgages were foreclosed, and the farms were abandoned. It was natural that these men should turn for relief toward the Government as the power strong enough to be of use. The Federal Government had given the land free to settlers, its army had protected them, its grants had made the Western railroads possible, it had given the settlers their territorial government and finally admitted them into the Union. And so the object of these discontented farmers was to get control of the Government or to force the Government to act in their behalf.

Their organization was ready at hand in the Granges and Farmers' Alliance, and the movement spread rapidly. Starting only in local politics, and not earlier than 1888, a national organization was first formed in 1891, and yet the People's Party polled over a million votes in 1892 and two years later nearly half a million more. The Populists demanded control by the Government, and if necessary Government ownership, of railroads, telegraphs, and telephones, the restoration to the Government of the excess lands granted to railroads, the abolition of the national banking system, the expansion of the national currency by the issue of *fiat* money and by the free and unlimited coinage of gold and silver in the ratio of 16 to 1, the establishment of postal savings banks, a graduated income tax, and the election of United States senators by direct vote of the people.

The Populist demands do not seem to us so very alarming; at the time they were characterized as revolutionary and anarchistic, but the extravagance of the language in which they were couched was partly responsible for that. In the Omaha platform of 1892 it was declared that "We meet in the midst of a nation brought to the verge of moral, political and material ruin. Corruption dominates the ballot box, the Legislatures, the Congress, and touches even the ermine of the Bench. The people are demoralized. . . . The fruits of the toil of millions are boldly stolen to build up colossal fortunes for a few. . . . From the same prolific womb of governmental injustice we breed the two great classes — tramps and millionaires." No wonder the conservative East was frightened and indiscriminately condemned whatever sprang from the "wild-eyed Populists." Perhaps it is too much to ask of those who are participating in an economic and political revolution, but if the men who were in power had only had some appreciation of the actual conditions and a little sympathy for the under dog, it might have saved a world of trouble later.

The first historian of the Populist movement, F. L. McVey, writing early in 1896, when the party was apparently in the full tide of prosperity, was inclined to criticize their cause and its platform, because "Every plank of any importance is an economic one and considers economic questions only. In fact, the whole movement might be designated as a protest against the present economic system." [1] President McVey was right, and yet the greater significance of the Populist uprising lay there, in the phenomenal growth of a party whose creed proclaimed its belief that it was the business of Government to regulate the economic concerns of life in the interests of the common people. In that doctrine, others were ready to join. For the farmer who, of necessity and yet of his own free will, worked in the fields from dawn to dark, it was hard to accept a declaration in the party platform in favor of an eight-hour day. For the sake of forming an alliance with labor, however, it was done, but it shows the fundamental character of the combination, that the Populists were a party of discontent.

Free silver
Unfortunately for the cause of reform the People's Party suddenly and too entirely laid emphasis upon free silver. A grievance of the West was the scarcity of money; this is a universal com-

[1] Frank L. McVey, "The Populist Movement," *Economic Studies*, American Economic Association, vol. I, no. 3 (1896), p. 187.

plaint, but in so far as it referred to a shortage of currency, to a scantiness in the medium of exchange, it expressed a genuine hardship and was characteristic of the frontier. When the United States was returning to a specie basis after the paper currency of the war, the Bland-Allison Act had been passed in 1878 providing for the purchase and coinage of from two to four million silver dollars every month. This was not enough to satisfy the demand and in connection with the passage of the McKinley Tariff Act, in 1890, the Western free silver men were strong enough to obtain further concessions, increasing the purchase to four and one half million ounces of silver every month, but not necessitating the coinage of this bullion. When the Panic of 1893 broke, President Cleveland, like many others of his countrymen, was so convinced that the Silver Purchase Act was largely responsible, that he forced a reluctant Congress in special session to repeal the objectionable act. At once a grievance was raised into an issue. With the confidence that is born of ignorance, many people in the country believed that the Government actually did create money by *fiat*, and the free coinage of silver became an obsession. "A fanaticism like that of the Crusades" spread through the West and became the feature of the presidential campaign of 1896.

One is apt to think of Mr. William J. Bryan, in the campaign of 1896, principally in connection with the closing sentences of his speech before the Democratic convention which secured him the nomination of that party: "We shall answer their demands for a gold standard by saying to them, you shall not press down upon the brow of labor this crown of thorns. You shall not crucify mankind upon a cross of gold." And the *New York World* expressed its disgust editorially: "Lunacy having dictated the platform it was perhaps natural that hysteria should evolve the candidate." In reality it is much nearer the truth to regard Mr. Bryan as being in hearty sympathy with his section of the country and, at thirty-six years of age, as giving expression to its needs with a whole-souled enthusiasm that made him the leader of all the discontented elements, as well as of the Democratic Party. It seems incredible now that a reputable New York paper could say: —

Its nominal head was worthy of the cause. Nominal, because the wretched, rattle-pated boy, posing in vapid vanity and mouthing resounding rottenness, was not the real leader of that league of hell. He was only a puppet in the blood-imbued hands of Altgeld, the anarchist, and Debs, the revolutionist, and other desperados of that stripe.[1]

---

[1] *New York Tribune*, editorial of November 6, 1896.

The language is extravagant even for an opponent in the excitement of a political campaign, but it must be remembered that to the conservative Eastern business man it seemed as if the Democratic platform and candidate were intended to undermine the very foundations of American prosperity. In that light the election of 1896 must be regarded. It was a combination of the big business interests of the country, under the leadership of Marcus A. Hanna, against a reform movement which seemed so radical as to be revolutionary and dangerous. William McKinley was chosen by Mark Hanna and the Republican Party as their nominee, and in the ensuing election he was successful, primarily because the immediate issue which the Democrats had raised was recognized as fallacious, and locally many votes were affected by a great rise in the price of wheat. Underneath was the larger reason that the country, generally prosperous, was not yet ready for the ideas of reform which were being advocated.

Nearly twenty years later, the New York *Nation* could write of Mr. Bryan and the free silver movement: "It may be argued, with considerable plausibility, that he builded better than he knew. Capitalistic interests really were guilty of great abuses, and Mr. Bryan, it may be argued, though wrong in the particular matter that he took hold of, stirred up a sentiment which, however ignorant, was righteous." If that be the case, as is now generally recognized, the election of 1896 would have been a temporary check only and not a defeat. The war with Spain, in 1898, diverted the attention of the people for a time, but no sooner was the war and its attendant questions settled than the spirit of discontent reasserted itself. In the meantime events had occurred which put an entirely different face on the situation. Large crops in the United States and a shortage in the world's markets carried the price of wheat to unprecedented figures. The discovery of gold in the Klondike and the development of African mines changed the silver question to one of gold and the complaint of low prices to a wail over the high cost of living.

High Finance
The culmination was reached in the era of "High Finance." The decade from 1887 to 1897 forms the period of the "trust in the strict legal sense," when large-scale production brought its foreordained results in further consolidation for the sake of the economies and advantages accruing from combination. The financial basis of the trust was the issuance of preferred stock or bonds representing the value of the constituent concerns, and of common stock capital-

izing the real or supposed profits resulting from elimination of competition. The prosperity of 1897 and 1898 not only had brought money to the public which it was eager to invest, but also had given unlimited confidence. There seemed to be no end, for "the profits of manufacture, notably in the steel and iron trades, went on increasing faster than promoters could turn their expectations into stock."

The growth of the steel industry has a romance of its own that reads like a tale of the Arabian Nights, but even that enterprise seemed to have overreached itself when J. Pierpont Morgan, the Wall Street leader in consolidation, formed the "billion-dollar steel trust" in March of 1901. Yet the rage for investment only grew into a mania, and April, 1901, was unparalleled in the history of the United States.

Not only did the younger men who had sold out to the Steel Corporation, now made into many times millionaires almost overnight and bewildered by their extraordinary fortune, toss into stock market ventures the money which they saw no other way of using, but old and experienced capitalists lost their heads, asserted publicly that the old traditions of finance no longer held and that a new order of things must now be reckoned with, and joined the dance. The "outside public," meantime, seemed to lose all restraint. A stream of excited customers, of every description, brought their money down to Wall Street, and spent their days in offices near the Stock Exchange. . . . The newspapers were full of stories of hotel waiters, clerks in business offices, even door-keepers and dressmakers, who had won considerable fortunes in their speculations.[1]

That the collapse of the bubble was not accompanied with more serious consequences is perhaps due to the fact that the Northern Pacific "corner" of May, 1901, frightened without badly hurting the general public, and that with the culmination in the "rich man's panic" of 1903, or even in that of 1907, the real bases of American prosperity were untouched.

These were the days of suddenly changing standards, of a great increase in the wealthy class and of a greater increase of individual fortunes, when the time of the millionaire passed and that of the multi-millionaire began. Expenditure rose on the same scale and was unrivaled in the experience of the United States. But it was reassuring to observe the old American spirit reasserting itself. Wealth that was so easily acquired lost something of its value and it was sought less and less for its own sake and more for what it represented and for its power. American generosity outdid itself. The world stood aghast at the lavish way with which money was spent, but it could not do otherwise than admire the stupendous phil-

[1] A. D. Noyes, *Forty Years of American Finance*, pp. 300–301.

anthropies which corresponded to the growth of fortunes, where one million was acceptable, but many millions were required to attract attention.

Concentration of industry was followed by the concentration of wealth; syndicates, interlocking directorates, and combinations in financial groups were the order of the day; one reads of the "Morgan interests" or of the "Standard Oil group." When one realizes the enormous power attaching to such accumulations of wealth and thinks of the insidious alliance that had grown up between business and politics, it will be seen that there was danger of, if there did not actually exist, a plutocracy,[1] and this was the situation with which the reawakened reform movement found itself confronted when the issues of the Spanish War became a thing of the past.

The new era   In a discussion several years ago among men who were prominent in their respective fields of business,

[1] "This was not all of it brought about by direct corruption, but much was effected through more insidious influence, and by furnishing the funds that political exigencies in important electoral contests called for. The time was, and we all know it, when in many of the directorates of the great corporations of the country, orders for the delivery of delegates in a convention and of members of the legislature for purposes of corporate control were issued with the same feeling of confidence in their fulfillment as an order for the purchase of machinery or the enlargement of the pay-roll." W. H. Taft, "The Signs of the Times," address before Electrical Manufacturers' Club, November 6, 1913, pp. 11–12.

politics, and professional life, the consensus of opinion showed itself to be that the outstanding features of American history since the Civil War were the concentration of industry and of wealth and the influence of business in politics. They were in the very midst of the reaction against these conditions and though keenly interested they were unable to define it or even to describe what was taking place. As we look back now it seems as if again an accident of history had largely affected the course of events. The assassination of McKinley at the beginning of his second term in 1901 placed in the presidential chair a man who was more quickly responsive to popular feeling, Mr. Theodore Roosevelt. If McKinley was, as he has been called, a political thermometer, Mr. Roosevelt was a political barometer, but he was more than that, as he helped to create the storms he foretold.

In the light of subsequent events it is amusing to read the new President's apparently sincere declaration that he would "continue absolutely unbroken the policy" of his predecessor. A strong believer in party organization he was evidently trying to keep the Republican machine in running order, and yet he was irresistibly diverted into becoming the leader of the reformers. In the presidential campaign of 1900 Mr. Bryan had thrust forward the question of imperialism, or the acquisition of the Philippines, and on that issue had been defeated. Two years later the President made a tour of New England and it was noted in the *Annual Register* that his speeches on imperialism aroused no interest whatever, but when he spoke on the tariff and the trusts the response was instantaneous. The question of the day could not be avoided and would not be evaded.

There is nothing to be gained by attacking or defending Mr. Roosevelt's course, and little except interest to be derived as yet from any attempt to describe his aggressive personality; the historian of the future must attend to that. But what he did cannot be passed by. In a clever sketch, which is a penetrating character study as well, the editor of the *Atlantic Monthly*, Mr. Ellery Sedgwick, framed an excellent introduction by saying: "Mr. Roosevelt was fortunate in the times in which he lived"; and the first point the writer emphasized was that "For seven years he preached as no revivalist ever preached on this continent. . . . From Wall Street to the ranges of the West his sermons were heard not one but seven days a week. Men listened and believed." [1] Whatever his motives, whatever his characteristics, Mr. Roosevelt became the mouthpiece of the

[1] *Atlantic Monthly*, May, 1912.

second generation, the exponent of its ideas, and the leader of its reforms.

The rapidity with which things happened, when combined with the instinct of the President for the dramatic, made the newspapers interesting to the reader of the day, but bewildering to the later student unless he holds fast to the main purpose of it all, and that was to break the hold of privilege and to weaken the power of wealth. The Interstate Commerce Commission had been established in 1887 at the time of the great awakening; its functions had been restricted by the courts largely to investigation; it had accomplished something in the way of publicity, and now, at Roosevelt's instigation, power was given "to determine and prescribe what will be the just and reasonable rates" for railroads. The Sherman Anti-Trust Law had been enacted in 1890 in response to the early excitement over the forming of combinations. It had been invoked successfully a few times and was now deliberately chosen as the instrument for attacking corporations that "were working to the public injury." Though only one of many, the most important of these cases resulted in the dissolution of the Northern Securities Company which had attempted a merger of the Northern Pacific and the Great Northern Railways. But the President was among the first to discriminate between good trusts and bad trusts, and in other cases as well furthered a policy that was not destructive, but constructive, and led upward to the "new nationalism" which demanded that the Government should meet the needs of the time and should take an active part in solving the new problems. This was admirably illustrated in the matter of conservation. The Newlands Act in 1902, for the reclamation of arid lands, and the forest reserve policy, having encountered opposition from private and corporate interests, pointed to the necessity of a more comprehensive plan for the conservation of the natural resources of the United States. This was well presented and so ably advocated, notably by Mr. Gifford Pinchot, that it has been an integral feature of American national policy, though not to the extent its supporters urged. The improvement of social conditions was still regarded as a matter rather for the individual states to handle.

The popularity of the President's course was attested in the election of 1904 when he won "the most sweeping victory in the history of American politics." Mr. Roosevelt accomplished much but, especially with a reluctant and even hostile Congress, he could not accomplish everything. Reforms were started, but were not completed; and one of his greatest services was the hope of better things he inspired. It was perhaps inevitable, after the turbulence of his seven years of office, that his successor, Mr. William Howard Taft, should suffer from the reaction just as Van Buren was punished for succeeding Jackson. Mr. Taft was a reformer, too, but he was not radical, and when it came to him to lead he allied with himself the conservative elements or the group that was called reactionary. With its assistance he did accomplish much in the way of advanced legislation, but not enough to satisfy the impatience of those who had now tasted of progress. "That leviathan, the people," to use one of Mr. Taft's favorite expressions, once aroused, started out on its independent career, blindly and blunderingly, but with unmistakable strength and power. In other words, the popular movement became the leading feature of the time and the part the individual played became subordinate. In childlike faith that laws were the one thing needful, direct legislation became the panacea and in the form of the initiative and referendum was introduced in many states. In order to strike at the heart of the political machine, or at least at the chiefs of the party organization, the popular election of United States senators was demanded. To accomplish this and to strike a blow at wealth by legalizing an income tax, the hitherto impossible was achieved in adopting two amendments to the Constitution. And to make assurance doubly sure nominations for office in many of the states were ordered to be reached through direct primaries.

There is a tradition of democracy in the United States which goes back to the real or imagined situation of nearly a hundred years ago. Absorbed in work, the people allowed an unhealthy state of affairs to develop, but always dreamed of reëstablishing former conditions, whenever they wished to do so. The time had come, but to their surprise the people found their will thwarted at almost every turn. In their anger they turned against any one and everything that opposed them. The judiciary is the most conservative of institutions and has served as a check on hasty popular impulse. The way in which it was resorted to by corporations under the Fourteenth Amendment has already been referred to, as well as to the resentment that was caused thereby. And now the people demanded a change. The form is immaterial; the popular election and recall of judges, and the so-called recall of judicial decisions, alike indicate an effort to force the judiciary to respond more quickly to public opinion. Yet the service which the conservative courts rendered was not slight. If no other, it gave time to bring a growing realization that the old democracy could never be restored.

The impatience of the reformers under a conservative policy led to an "insurgent" Republican opposition in Congress, which in coöperation with the Democrats succeeded in 1910 in breaking the power of the Speaker, but, be it said, without increasing the efficiency of the House. The movement was supported by the more ardent of the Roosevelt faction and finally by Mr. Roosevelt himself. The conservative elements of the party were still in control of the machine and in the convention of 1912 prevented the nomination of Mr. Roosevelt and secured the renomination of Mr. Taft. Mr. Roosevelt and his supporters thereupon broke away and formed the new Progressive Party, embodying the spirit of progress which has been described as animating the second generation, and comprising a medley of reformers and discontented elements. The split in the Republican Party was probably responsible for the election of the Democratic candidate, Governor Woodrow Wilson, but although the country was desirous of progressive measures, it seems to have been tired of being preached at and welcomed the chance of a quiet administration. The Progressive Party met the fate of all third-party movements since the Civil War, for its real mission was accomplished by its show of strength in forcing the older parties to accept and carry out its reforms. There is truth in the saying that the great service of the Progressive Party was in making "socialistic ideas" respectable.

Just before his election as Governor of New Jersey in 1910, Mr. Wilson is reported to have said that "I understand the principles of the campaign to mean this, that if I am elected Governor I shall have been elected leader of my party." It was primarily as leader of the Democratic Party that he acted in his first administration as President of the United States, which will probably long remain with an unequaled record of legislative achievement, and for this the greatest credit must be given to Mr. Wilson himself. Merely to mention a substantial reduction in tariff rates, a revision of the banking and currency system, the strengthening of the Interstate Commerce Commission, bolstering up the anti-trust acts, and creating a Federal Trade Commission, would be sufficient to indicate accomplishment, but not to reveal the character of what was taking place. These and other acts meant a strengthening of federal authority at the expense of local governments, contrary to Jeffersonian theories of democracy. But in the face of the exigencies of fact Mr. Wilson has been as disregardful of theory and of his own preconceived doctrines as was Jefferson himself when he became President. The industrial democracy of to-day must rest upon another basis than the landed democracy of earlier times. It is too soon to pass judgment upon the merits of what was done or to analyze the results of the election of 1916, but it seems, even with the dissatisfaction which his first term aroused, as if, in the opinion of the people, Mr. Wilson had accomplished more in the direction of positive reform than was likely under a conservative Republican leadership.

BIBLIOGRAPHY

Two books will be found especially helpful for the subjects of this chapter: H. T. Peck, *Twenty Years of the Republic, 1885–1905* (1907), and F. A. Ogg, *National Progress* (1918). Biographies and autobiographies are indispensable. The best are Herbert Croly, *Marcus Alonzo Hanna* (1912), C. Lloyd, *Henry Demarest Lloyd* (2 vols., 1912), *Theodore Roosevelt, an Autobiography* (1913), R. M. LaFollette, *A Personal Narrative of Political Experiences* (1913), S. W. McCall, *Life of Thomas B. Reed* (1914), and W. R. Thayer, *Life and Letters of John Hay* (2 vols., 1915).

Among the works on special subjects to be recommended are I. M. Tarbell, *The Tariff in Our Times* (1911), C. R. Van Hise, *Conservation of Natural Resources of the United States* (1910), Alexander D. Noyes, *Forty Years of American Finance* (1898, with subsequent editions), Brooks Adams, *The Theory of Social Revolutions* (1913), A. T. Hadley, *Undercurrents in American Politics* (1915), and F. L. Paxson, "The Rise of Sport" in *Mississippi Valley Historical Review* (1917).

CHAPTER XVI

THE UNITED STATES AS A WORLD POWER

In spite of the recognition grudgingly accorded the proclamation of the Monroe Doctrine early in the nineteenth century, the United States did not become a power in world affairs outside of the American continents, although the country's growth to economic independence and then to industrial importance was necessarily accompanied by some show of consideration from others. The outcome of the Civil War, however, raised the Federal Government in general estimation and events immediately subsequent still further increased the world's respect.

The French in Mexico Napoleon III had thought that he saw an opportunity to regain for France a foothold upon the western continent and took advantage of America's absorption in the war to intervene in Mexico, where, in 1863, he established the Archduke Maximilian of Austria as emperor. The venture was not proving successful, as it could be maintained only with troops and money, which France could ill afford, especially in view of Germany's aggressiveness. The American Secretary of State, William H.

Seward, was an able diplomat and simply awaited his opportunity. At the right moment he insisted upon the withdrawal of the French troops and, in 1866, Napoleon yielded, greatly to the credit of the United States and of American diplomacy.

Alaska Again during the Civil War there had been considerable probability of foreign intervention, or at least of a demonstration against the Northern blockade of the Southern ports. Rumor has it that the United States sought out some power to come to the support of the Federal Government, that the Russian navy appeared in American waters at a critical time, and that the payment of five million dollars for this service was covered in the purchase of Alaska for $7,500,000 in 1867. Whatever may be the truth or lack of truth in this story — and the charge would seem to be excessive for the old hulks that the Russians are said to have sent — there is every reason for considering the taking of Alaska off Russia's hands as a friendly act. The purchase was commonly referred to as "Seward's Folly," and it is entertaining, especially in view of subsequent developments, to read that some tried to find justification by claiming that Americans were thwarting the plans of the British, and that, anyway, Alaska would simply round off the northern continental possessions, as of course eventually Canada would become a part of the United States.

Expatriation
There was also obtained at this time a solution of the old and perplexing problem of naturalization, which had been left unsettled by the War of 1812. The increase of immigration to the United States after 1840 repeatedly brought up the practical question of whether any person had the right to renounce allegiance to one country and become the citizen or subject of another, and as the largest numbers of immigrants were coming from Ireland and the German states, difficulties arose most frequently in connection with those countries. Shortly before the war, a naturalized citizen of the United States, returning to his birthplace in Hanover, was arrested and forced into the army, and though, upon strong American representations, the Hanoverian Government stated that "a full pardon had been granted" and that the man in question "had been dismissed from the military service," this was not a recognition of the principle contended for. The trouble with the British reached its climax just after the war through the Fenian agitations and the arrest of naturalized American citizens who were natives of Ireland. Anti-British sentiments being strongly in the ascendant in the United States, stirring resolutions

were passed by both political parties and a federal statute of July, 1868, formally declared that "expatriation is a natural and inherent right of all people, indispensable to the enjoyment of the rights of life, liberty, and the pursuit of happiness." This was only a bit of political buncombe, as several months before the United States Minister to Prussia, George Bancroft, had concluded a naturalization treaty with the North German Union, followed soon after by treaties with South German states, and there was every reason to expect in the immediate future similar treaties would be made with other powers, including Great Britain. Still it did not lessen the achievement of having obtained general acceptance of the principles for which the United States had contended usually against the rest of the world.

The Alabama Claims But the greatest increase of American prestige resulted from the Treaty of Washington, in 1871, which was of itself a noteworthy event in international relations, as Great Britain and the United States referred all of the main questions at issue between them to peaceful arbitration and judicial settlement. Other matters were important and yet were insignificant in comparison with the award of the Geneva Tribunal. Constituted to consider the particular question, it granted damages of $15,000,000 to the United States for Great Britain's relaxation of neutrality in allowing the Alabama and other ships to sail from British ports and prey upon federal commerce. The damages may have been excessive; they were so regarded by Englishmen at the time, though promptly paid, and when the Americans came to divide the amount among the direct claimants, a balance was left over, a part of which was distributed among the insurance companies whose claims had been thrown out by the Geneva Tribunal; but this in no way detracted from the importance of the position to which the United States had attained.

American diplomacy All of these occurrences brought increased respect for the power of the United States, and yet Americans in general kept aloof from the affairs of the world and so remained peculiarly backward in their interest in international matters and in their concern for foreign relations. Occasional Presidents might have efficient Secretaries of State, but the mass of the people regarded diplomacy as an adjunct of monarchy and diplomatic usages as unworthy of observance. The attitude of the people was fairly represented by Congress, which refused to make adequate grants to American representatives at foreign courts, and if they maintained among their fellow diplomats positions worthy of their status, they did so at their own expense. It was not until 1893 that Congress finally gave its consent to appointments of the grade of ambassador, and even then it was smuggled into a clause in an appropriation act, permitting the President to reciprocate when another power sent an ambassador to the United States. De Tocqueville pointed out that equality was the ultimate basis of good manners, and so it was with American diplomacy, which had sunk to a low ebb. The disregard of formal observances was largely due to the ignorance of provincialism and to lack of experience, but in the long run American principles of open dealing, fair play, and consideration for others were bound to improve diplomatic intercourse. Until this was achieved, and it required time, it is not unnatural that foreign governments should have looked down upon American diplomacy, and that Washington should have been regarded neither as an important nor as an attractive diplomatic post.

Venezuela, 1895 It was, therefore, a surprise to the world and a shock to the British when in 1895 the United States suddenly demanded, in accordance with the Monroe Doctrine, that a boundary dispute, of which most people had never heard, between Great Britain and Venezuela, should be settled by arbitration. It hardly seemed as if that doctrine applied in this case, and Lord Salisbury, the British Foreign and Prime Minister, said as much in declining to arbitrate. He failed to appreciate how the American people cherish the Monroe Doctrine. Deep in their hearts it lies as an expression of Americanism, defensive at the time it was uttered, in that European systems would have been dangerous to the peace and safety of the United States, and later idealized because it was also altruistic, an older and stronger nation protecting the interests of younger and weaker states. And one of the best things about the Monroe Doctrine, from the standpoint of the United States, is its indefiniteness or its elasticity, which makes it applicable to any situation.

On receiving the British reply, President Cleveland recommended to Congress, in a special message, the appointment of a commission to determine for itself the true boundary line in dispute. When Congress passed a bill appropriating a hundred thousand dollars for this commission, without a single dissenting vote in either house, and was supported by public opinion throughout the United States, and when all England stood aghast at the prospect of war, Lord Salisbury saw his mistake and tactfully permitted the American commission to have the benefit of British information with access to British official records. Before this commission could make its report, arbitration was agreed to and a board appointed, whose decision was accepted by all parties. The language which the American Government had used was not the ordinary language of diplomacy, but there was no mistaking its meaning. Great Britain had yielded on the principle involved, and the American people were proud of their President and proud of themselves, while to their astonishment they found themselves on better terms with the British than ever before, because the result of the incident was an increased mutual respect.

On the other hand, in spite of good intentions the action of the United States was not popular in South America, partly because the North American and the Southern Latin types had failed to understand each other, but largely because of the misconception by Richard Olney, the Secretary of State, of the conditions and relations between the states of North and South America. According to Professor Fish, more errors could hardly have been compressed into fewer words than in Olney's remark that "the states of America,

South as well as North, by geographical proximity, by natural sympathy, by similarity of governmental institutions, are friends and allies, commercially and politically, of the United States." [1] Nor was the strain of the situation relieved by his further statement that "To-day the United States is practically sovereign on this continent, and its fiat is law upon the subjects to which it confines its interposition."

War with Spain In 1898 the United States went to war with Spain over conditions in Cuba for reasons that were "partly commercial, partly hysterical, and partly humanitarian." It was only a four-months war and the losses in action were numbered by tens of officers and hundreds of men, though reliance upon a volunteer system brought the usual heavy toll, which unpreparedness of the army entails, in that the deaths from typhoid fever alone were several times greater than those in battle. The war with Spain may have been insignificant in its fighting, but it was impressive in its consequences. The best traditions of the navy were maintained and their glory strengthened. There were the usual war accompaniments of enthusiasm and patriotism as great as the size of the contest warranted, but of no

[1] *American Diplomacy*, p. 395.

greater significance than the disappearance of a former sectionalism. This was illustrated in the story told of the ex-Confederate officer who now volunteered to fight under the United States flag, but forgot himself in the excitement of the charge and called to his men, "Come on! Kill the damned Yanks!"

But the greatest importance attaches to the position attained by the United States and the recognition accorded by other powers. There is some question as to the exact service and by whom rendered, when an attempt was made before the outbreak of hostilities to isolate the United States diplomatically, but there is no doubt that the attempt was thwarted and there is also no doubt of the marked friendliness of the British Government. John Hay, the American Ambassador, wrote home from London: "If we wanted it . . . we could have the practical assistance of the British navy — on the *do ut des* principle, naturally." When this was not made use of, the British strained the bonds of international usage to extend courtesies to the Americans that were of very practical assistance. Though no official recognition could be taken of this service, it remained among the traditions of the Republican Party, and was doubtless partly responsible for the hurt feeling of the British, at the outbreak of the Great War, when the Americans did not show any disposition to return the "courtesies" which had been extended to them years before.

Americans have no reason to be ashamed of their intervention in Cuba, in spite of European skepticism, for there seems to have been no thought of annexation and only a jealous fear lest the young republic should not justify American confidence. There were acquisitions of territory, however, as a result of the war that were more or less unexpected. The incorporation of the Hawaiian Islands in the United States was a foregone conclusion, and, though it had not been previously possible to get a President and two-thirds of the Senate in accord as to a treaty, the exigencies of war brought a joint resolution for annexation, which was just as effective and required only a majority vote. Porto Rico and the Philippines were spoils of war. "Mr. Dooley" said rightly of his countrymen that when they first heard of the Philippines they thought it was a breakfast food. But while negotiations for peace were under way President McKinley made a tour of the South and West and to his surprise found the sentiment of those sections strongly in favor of annexation. He accordingly instructed the commissioners in Paris to insist upon the retention of these islands and an indemnity therefor of twenty million dollars was granted. It marked the beginning of a new epoch in the foreign relations of the United States, for it meant the recognition by the American people themselves, as well as by the rest of the world, that their country had risen to be a world power in the accepted use of that expression.

An interesting feature of the new development was that Americans had apparently departed from their original and cherished colonial system by acquiring territory which was not to be incorporated, on a footing of equality, into the Union of states. In fact the idea of incorporation was so fixed in the minds of Americans that many actually questioned the constitutional right to acquire territory which was not to become a state. They overlooked the precedent of Alaska, and they failed to see that their position was exactly the reverse of what it had been at the time of the Louisiana Purchase in 1803, when the promise of incorporation was declared not merely unwise but illegal.

The Far East In spite of themselves the Americans had already been drawn outside of the American continents and sooner or later they would have been forced into taking their rightful place in the affairs of the world. The United States had been responsible for the opening of Japan to foreign commerce, and had coöperated with European powers in several instances in Pacific Ocean affairs, notably in the settlement of the Samoan question in 1889. By virtue of their commercial and industrial activities the Americans were rising to a position of world importance, and it was an accident of history that they assumed that place through the Spanish War. Their growing interest in trade and their missionary work in the Far East would have made them want to share in the intervention in China at the time of the Boxer troubles in 1900, and the fact that they were already in the Philippines simply made it possible for them to act with greater effectiveness.

We have no choice, we people of the United States, as to whether or not we shall play a great part in the world. That has been determined for us by fate, by the march of events. We have to play that part. All that we can decide is whether we shall play it well or ill.

President Roosevelt's words were prophetic as well as retrospective, especially in reference to American relations with the Orient. The treatment accorded to the Chinese and Japanese in California and other Pacific Coast States, culminating in an exclusion policy, might leave something to be desired, but is understandable when we remember that "competition between races is a competition in standards of living," and Americans may well take pride in many things their Government has done in the Far East. In 1864 the United States hired a little vessel that it might share with Great Britain, France, and Holland in the bombardment to punish Japan for closing the straits of Shimonoseki, and it received a fourth of the indemnity, only to have Congress, twenty years later, restore its share to Japan. When war broke out between China and Japan in 1894 each belligerent gave its interests in the other country into the care of the United States. After the Boxer troubles in China John Hay, then Secretary of State, successfully carried through the recognition of the "open door" policy which was representative of the new diplomacy of the United States and probably prevented the dismemberment of China. Although the compensation of $24,000,000, obtained for damages sustained in the rebellion, seemed moderate in comparison with the demands of some of the other powers, the United States retained only the amount necessary to meet the actual losses suffered and returned the balance of $14,000,000 to China, in 1907. It was the refinement of courtesy that permitted China to show its appreciation by dedicating this fund to the education of Chinese students in the United States.

Roose-
velt in
foreign
relations
President Roosevelt's administration set a new record for America's participation in foreign affairs, some diplomats regarding him as a genius in his instinct for comprehending a situation and for acting as circumstances demanded. Other nations could understand, as many Americans could not, his method of bringing the Germans to arbitrate the Venezuelan matter in 1902 by an intimation of force. The acquisition of the Panama Canal Zone in 1903 was a high-handed action, of which many have not been able to approve; but the story of the revolution fostered by M. Bunau-Varilla from a fashionable hotel in New York City reads like opéra bouffe, and when all the circumstances are taken into account it is hard to condemn what was done, especially in view of a completed Isthmian canal. The position which the United States and its President attained is shown by their serving as the place of negotiation and mediator to end the war between Russia and Japan in 1905, by the part that was taken in the Algeciras Conference of 1906, and by the growing appreciation of the responsibilities as well as of the privileges under the Monroe Doctrine. States could not be allowed to shirk the consequences

of their acts, and in order to prevent foreign intervention the United States took San Domingo under its guardianship until it should pay its just debts.

Peace-keeping Although the United States has been by no means entirely exempt, it has been, in comparison with most of the other powers, remarkably free from war, and has been engaged in none which could in any way be regarded as a great contest, except for its own struggle to preserve the Union. For over a hundred years the United States has remained at peace with England and an unfortified boundary has sufficed to mark the line of separation from Canada. The Americans have long advocated, and were among the earliest to use, arbitration in the settlement of disputes. They took a prominent part in the various peace conferences at The Hague; they referred the first case to the permanent court of arbitration at The Hague for trial; and they have been one of the leading nations to submit their causes to peaceful methods of decision, for they are lovers of peace. In his *Contributions of the United States to Civilization*, President Eliot laid emphasis upon arbitration as one of these; this the late Senhor Nabuco, the Brazilian Ambassador to the United States, was not willing to accept unless it were taken in the sense of peace-keeping, when he said, "It has been one of your mightiest contributions to civilization." [1]

Mexico So it was that the American people as a whole supported President Wilson in his determination to keep out of war with Mexico. While Great Britain and European powers evinced a willingness to allow the United States a free hand in its dealing with a situation of anarchy, there was a growing disposition to hold Americans responsible for results which might have necessitated action and precipitated important consequences, if the Great War had not broken out and upset all calculations. Whatever criticisms may be made of the President's course and apparent inconsistency, it would seem as if the relations of the United States with its Spanish American neighbors have been put upon a better footing and that in place of the Monroe Doctrine, with distrust ever attendant upon it, a more generally acceptable Pan-American doctrine may emerge.

The Great War So it was, also, that the American people supported President Wilson in his efforts to keep out of the European struggle. Sufficient cause for fighting had been given over and over again, but everything was borne, not so much for

[1] "Share of America in Civilization," *American Historical Review*, October, 1909.

the profits of neutrality as that the people longed to be allowed to remain at peace. More and more Americans, however, were learning to appreciate that the cause of the Allies was their own, and, when the limit of endurance was finally reached, Mr. Wilson found that his methods and policy had resulted in a more united people backing him than the United States had ever had in going to war before. His countrymen support him whole-heartedly and are proud of the way in which their President has unmistakably shown their disinterested purposes and that in expressing the hopes of American idealism he has formulated the issues of peace for the world.

In 1907 there was fear, if not actual danger, of war between Japan and the United States. As a demonstration of power, or at any rate as a precautionary measure, President Roosevelt sent the American fleet on its memorable voyage around the world. It was not a pleasure cruise, and for the sake of the training, if for no other reason, the ships sailed as though ready for action at any moment. European powers did not believe that the fleet could get to the Pacific, but its success settled the question. It may have been absurd, yet there were those who thought that Japan might have made a surprise attack, especially upon the unprotected Pacific Coast of the United States, which would probably have been successful, and they feared that the Americans would never rest until they had inflicted a crushing defeat in return. Under the circumstances it would have necessitated turning their resources and devoting their strength to one purpose until the whole United States had become a great fighting machine. And that is now happening. Germany drove the United States into the war against its will, and once in there is no holding back. Democracy is apt to proceed slowly and blunderingly; and in this instance the immediate achievements were disappointing to Americans as well as to the Allies. There were mistakes and unwise moves, and the wasting of precious time, but measures were adopted that a few years before were undreamed of and only a few months before would have been impossible.

For years many Americans were disturbed over the excessive immigration into the United States because, great as the powers of absorption might be, it seemed as if the point of saturation had been reached. The situation was similar to that at the time of the Revolution. The outbreak of the European war caused serious dissensions in American public opinion as was natural in a people of whose blood it is estimated that one fifth is German. But there were compensating elements, such as the stopping of immigration, and when the United States entered the war great unifying forces began to work. The compulsory service law, with its mingling of millions of men in the training camps, the coöperation of the entire people in active support and in voluntary self-denial, the consciousness of the common effort and the sharing of the common sorrows, are accomplishing in a short time what ordinarily requires years or even generations. Racial and national differences are forgotten, while sectional prejudices are ignored and class interests are overlooked in order that a united people may put forth the ultimate and unknown strength of the whole United States.

Yet there is no danger of a militant nation resulting, for this is not inspired by love of fighting. It is a self-reliant people rising to meet an emergency, and as Americans have followed only their traditions and their training, so they will return to their former ways. Out of the educational and industrial systems of the United States, college men, professional men, and the chief business men, as well as individuals of wealth and leisure, offered themselves for service in work of any sort and in the ranks if need be, but they have risen to leadership and are directing the energies of a nation. These same trained minds far-sightedly are planning a later reconstruction in which warfare has no part. They are basing those plans upon experience, but they are making them with a broader outlook, with quickened sympathies, and with a new sense of their responsibility especially in international affairs.

BIBLIOGRAPHY

Almost all of the narrative histories treat of the subject of foreign relations more or less satisfactorily. Special works to be recommended are C. R. Fish, *American Diplomacy* (1915), J. B. Moore, *American Diplomacy* (1905; revised edition, 1918), J. B. Henderson, *American Diplomatic Questions* (1901), J. H. Latané, *America as a World Power, 1897–1907* (1907), A. C. Coolidge, *United States as a World Power* (1908), and F. E. Chadwick, *Relations of the United States and Spain, 1776–1898*: Vol. I, *Diplomacy*, (1909), Vols. II and III, *Spanish American War* (1911).

INDEX

INDEX

343